Y0-BVP-151

A15043 406066

19

Occasional Paper Series

Terrorism:

Pragmatic
International Deterrence
and Cooperation

Richard Allan

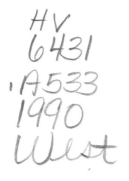

Institute for East-West Security Studies
New York · 1990

WESTVIEW PRESS * BOULDER, COLORADO

The Institute for East-West Security Studies does not take or
encourage specific policy positions. It is committed to encouraging and facilitating the discussion of important issues of concern to East and West. The views expressed in this report do not
necessarily reflect the opinions of the Board of Directors, the
officers or the staff of the Institute.

Distributed by Westview Press
          Frederick A. Praeger, Publisher
          5500 Central Avenue
          Boulder, Colorado 80301

Library of Congress Cataloging-in-Publication Data

Allan, Richard, 1931-
     Terrorism : pragmatic international deterrence and cooperation /
Richard Allan.
          p.   cm. — (Occasional paper series : 19)
     Includes bibliographical references.
     ISBN 0-913449-22-9 (IEWSS) : $12.85. — ISBN 0-8133-8132-0 (Westview) :
$12.85
     1. Terrorism.   2. Terrorism—Prevention—Government policy—United
States. 3. Terrorism—Prevention—Government policy.   4. Extradition.
     I. Title.   II. Series: Occasional paper series (Institute for East-West Secu-
rity Studies) : 19.
     HV6431.A533   1990
     363.3'2—dc20   90-19705
                                                                         CIP

CONTENTS

FOREWORD

The threat of large-scale conventional conflict in Europe may have diminished because of Eastern Europe's major changes in 1989, but violent struggle is still an element of today's political lexicon. As this book is published, large standing armies face each other in the Arabian Peninsula. Perhaps even more ominously, armed terrorists continue to plot violence against innocent civilians.

The challenge of containing terrorism is rapidly becoming as important as containment of conventional and nuclear threats to the preservation of international security. This issue is squarely addressed by Richard Allan, professor of law at Brooklyn Law School in New York and 1989–91 American Scholar-in-Residence at the Institute for East-West Security Studies.

Professor Allan's intention in writing this paper was not to seek or project a consensus for a particular method of confronting terrorism, nor did he merely present the issues in a Socratic form. Rather, Professor Allan hopes that this paper will generate a focused and precisely defined discussion on pragmatic issues that will lead to a non-theoretical and viable method of containment.

Professor Allan does not for a moment argue that an attack on a government building, installation or official is not a crime. But it is an attack of a different physical and psychological nature than an attack on a school bus filled with children or an airport filled with holiday travelers. A police officer or military person is never a civilian so long as he or she is "attached", in or out of uniform, to a government. The assassination of a government minister may be a political statement of a repressed society; the murder of a family returning from work, or on a holiday picnic, or weekend outing can never be a political statement. Therefore, the book narrows the definition of terrorism and focuses only on violence against a civilian population, so that we may formulate a step-by-step concerted response by all nations. Certain questions are not addressed in this book: What about a situation where the target is not a civilian? When should an attack be termed the work of a freedom fighter, guerrilla, criminal, or "political" terrorist? Such issues must be left for another discussion.

We must move away from a situation in which each nation views terrorism through its own political or social prism. To this end, Professor Allan advocates the use of the International Court of Justice as a means of committing all nations to one unified extradition procedure for those accused of terrorism as narrowly defined in this book. The author also proposes a system of electronic surveillance of a segment of the terrorist population. This will serve to prevent the use of "sleepers" to create havoc within a society, while recognizing both the need for security *and* the protection of individual civil rights during this process.

Professor Allan graciously credits many individuals with assistance in his work, and has asked to acknowledge them in his own words:

"The IEWSS and its fellows have been wonderfully supportive during my writing of this paper. Brooklyn Law School, my professional home since 1973, not only financed my sabbatical so that I could spend my time at the IEWSS, but has encouraged my travel into this non-traditional area of law school study. I would also like to thank Maurice Klein, of the Canadian Security Intelligence Review Committee, for his guidance in the section on Canada's system of surveillance oversight. Lastly, there are three people I must acknowledge: Lee Allan, my wife, who took my initial volumes of material and edited and rearranged their mass to get this paper completed. She was followed by an old and dear friend, Professor Marvin Magalaner, who must have had an easier time writing his many volumes of criticism, and finally, Rosalie Kearns, the Institute's Publications Editor, who quizzed me on every sentence of the entire paper."

The Institute would also like to express its gratitude to the following philanthropic foundations for their generous support of IEWSS programs: The Carnegie Corporation of New York; The Ford Foundation; The William and Flora Hewlett Foundation; The Alfried Krupp von Bohlen und Halbach-Foundation; The John D. and Catherine T. MacArthur Foundation; The McKnight Foundation; The Rockefeller Family and Associates; The Rockefeller Foundation; The Scherman Foundation; The Florence and John Schumann Foundation; and the Weyerhaeuser Foundation, Inc.

In addition, the Institute would like to thank Richard Levitt, Director of Publications, and Jeff Hoover, Publications Associate, for their work on this book.

The author and I both hope that this book will prompt discussion and reflection that will ultimately influence balanced policies to contain terrorism. We worry that policies of reaction, not those of reflection, all too often produce doomsday legislation and ineffective responses. For all the work that has gone before in this growing field of academic study, there will always be room for a well-reasoned and thoughtful contribution, such as the author has provided.

John Edwin Mroz
President
December 1990

INTRODUCTION

The magnitude of the threat of international terrorism is unknown. Western governments purport to assure their own populations that there is vigilance and protection; nevertheless, hostages remain in captivity, the rewards offered for information leading to interdiction of this crime have increased dramatically,[1] and the frequency of official warnings of potential terrorist attacks has escalated.[2] The international community, notwithstanding its claimed successes, has failed to adequately arrest, prosecute, and, if necessary, extradite those responsible for terrorism.

Terrorism is not a momentary phenomenon. On the contrary—current evidence indicates that both the diversity and amount of terrorism will increase. What is required is a focus on the word *terrorism* that permits international policy makers to move forward beyond the mere exchange of information and toward international cooperation, utilizing extradition, the International Court of Justice, and extended domestic electronic surveillance of the terrorist as a "sleeper".

Low-intensity conflict or *alternative means of violence* are but two of several terms used as euphemisms for the word *terrorism*, a word imbued with immense psychological impact, a word full of pejorative connotations, implying brutal and savage conduct outside the accepted rules of conflict.[3] Worldwide,

---

1. The United States has increased the amount of the reward it offers to $4 million to those persons who provide information that stops an act of terrorism.
2. In late October, the State Department issued an unusually explicit warning of a possible terrorist attack, not against an airline or public or military installation, but against a passenger ship. *The New York Times*, October 27, 1990, p. 4.
3. The prevailing view appears to hold that UN Charter article 2(4) prohibits any significant use of force unless its utilization is justified by one of a limited number of exceptions contained in the charter or by customary international law (e.g., the right to self-defense) or article 51 of the charter; see Roda Mushkat, "When War May Justifiably be Waged," *Brooklyn Journal of International Law* 15, no. 2 (1989), p. 223. There is an important distinction between laws of armed conflict, i.e., rules governing all armed

neither the political right nor left has the dubious distinction of claiming exclusive monopoly of international terrorism as a method to promote its causes. Nor has society generally condemned acts of terrorism merely because of their destructive and violent impact, for then a fortiori all violence would be unconditionally condemned. And although an ultimate goal of the United Nations is that each nation "refrain in their international relations from the threat or use of force,"[4] in reality, non-nuclear confrontation is a possible and, at times, internationally acceptable method of conduct between opposing forces.[5]

Terrorism's prime purpose, whether motivated by political, religious, social, economic or racial conflict, is to create public recognition for its creator and his or her claims and causes. Given the nature of a terrorist act—random selection of targets, unique means of delivering violence, unpredictability—its intended results will create immediate and immense shock within a population. Perpetrators then hope that the shock will develop into public hysteria.[6] The target government is then perceived as being either ineffective, negligent or, at the very least, unacceptable. Eventually, the very moral fiber of a political and social system becomes overstretched and fragile, and the slightest tremor to the structure of a government or the continued threat to personal safety of a population produces major outbursts of extreme irrational behavior in the name of "containment" of terrorism and "safety" from violence. An example of this behavior on the part of a government is the suspension of the right to habeas corpus proceeding by the British Parliament in a response to terrorism in Northern Ireland. Terrorism can, under certain circumstances, shake the

---

conflict by all nations, and rules of engagement, i.e., rules established by a single government to govern armed conflict by its own armed forces at a particular time and place. It is internationally accepted that rules of engagement cannot supercede laws of armed conflict.
4. UN Charter, article 2 (4). (See Appendix B.)
5. Christopher Greenwood, "International Law and The United States Air Operation Against Libya," *West Virginia Law Review* 89 (1987), p. 993. See also Appendix B for the text of the Resolution of the UN Security Council, which is interpreted by some to authorize *military* action to halt all maritime trade with Iraq: "measures commensurate to the specific circumstances. . .to halt all. . .maritime shipping."
6. David Rapoport, "The Politics of Atrocity," *Terrorism: Interdisciplinary Perspectives* (New York: John Jay College Press, 1977).

very framework of a weak, young or inexperienced government, when the enormity or repetition of acts of violence affects the accepted psychological relationships between the state governing body and its electorate.[7] Any security system, whether cast as a law, theory or operational formula, cannot be permitted to be a national or international reflection of shock and anger initiated by violent events. It must develop as a rational process compatible with democratic restraints and obligations.

Now, during a relatively calm period,[8] a time without undue public pressure to respond immediately to the violence of terrorism, a time when all the major powers profess a desire for accommodation, a plan for coping with terrorism must be developed and put in place. Although there has been some success in the containment of terrorism, the legal and intelligence tools presently available have not adequately contained either the threat or actual explosion of violence. The strategies adopted must be preventive, not executed in response to the devastation and anger produced by bombings, kidnapping and murder: "A country under direct attack will prefer to err on the side of overreaction."[9] The pragmatic international cooperation necessary to more effectively contain this criminal behavior has been prevented by disagreement over definitions of the words *terrorist* and *terrorism* and the classification of targets.

In chapter 1 of this paper I will utilize a legal and political analysis to understand the scope of terrorism and the present failure to move toward greater containment. Crucial to any program of containment is the necessity to first define the word

---

7. See Ronald Crelinsten, "Terrorism, Counter-Terrorism and Democracy," *Terrorism and Political Violence* 1, no. 2 (1989), p. 243.
8. The lull in terrorist activity directed from the Middle East may end shortly with the Iraqi invasion of Kuwait and the US military intervention in Saudi Arabia in August 1990. It has been reported that several Palestinian terrorist organizations are actively planning attacks against US targets on behalf of Iraq. "Most but not all of the Palestinian organizations are involved" in planning attacks against American interests. "These people are offering their services free to Iraq." Abul Abbas, interviewed by *The Wall Street Journal*, September 10, 1990, p. 1, indicated that terrorism is a necessary part of Saddam Hussein's war, and that Hussein has been joined in Baghdad by Abu Nidal. On September 12, 1990, Iran's supreme religious leader called for all Muslims to exercise their religious duty to wage a "holy war" against the US because of its deployment of troops in the Gulf region. *International Herald Tribune*, September 13, 1990, p. 1.
9. Walter Laqueur, *The Age of Terrorism* (Boston: Little Brown, 1987), p. 311.

terrorism in a way that permits policy makers to move beyond continued discussion of its meaning and to formulate specific pragmatic operational plans. I have developed a definition that clearly focuses on a narrow spectrum of violence.

Terrorism, however defined, will not disappear unless a totally oppressive state is in place, and all forms of expression are subjected to censorship.[10] Such a state would also have to set up a spying mechanism to ferret out potential dissidents, who would then be involuntarily removed from the general society to a less sensitive environment. Consequently, in a society with an open form of government, terrorism can only be contained, at best. The purpose of chapters 2 and 3 of this paper is to suggest and explore two related methods to attain the goal of reducing the continued mistrust and international political clashes created by an international terrorist incident. This goal must be met without an extreme intrusion into the sovereignty of a state or a restriction on the freedom of expression and association by individuals.

It is proposed in chapter 2 that, through international cooperation, the grounds for international extradition be made neutral, while retaining the use of the political exception rule for those whose extradition is sought for non-terrorist violence. This proposal calls for narrowing the political exception rule, which supports a claim by a defendant that his or her common criminal act was either politically motivated or was committed in a political context and, therefore, he or she has not committed an extraditable crime. The proposal would prevent fallacious exploitation of the international extradition process. The proposal discussed in chapter 3 is a corollary to the first, and calls for a narrowly defined but liberal use of electronic surveillance in the United States, aimed at potential "sleepers," i.e., persons who are introduced legally into a country to become assimilated by a community while awaiting orders, which may come months or years after arrival, for the sole purpose of performing an act of terrorism.

Notwithstanding the extraordinary public access to weapons and explosives in the United States, and the absolute freedom of travel between the states by any person, there is no fully satisfactory explanation of why the US has been exception-

---

10. See Jean-Francois Revel, *How Democracies Perish* (New York: Harper & Row, 1983).

ally free of the volume of successful international terrorism experienced by other nations (such as France, Spain, West Germany, Turkey, Peru).[11] That may change in the 1990s. The acts of violence within the United States that can be defined as purely domestic terrorism have been initiated by separatist groups such as the Macheteros in Puerto Rico,[12] or the fringe elements of indigenous groups such as the animal rights and pro-life movements.

I recognize that individuals and fringe groups are not the only sources of terrorist violence: the World War II mass bombings of cities, which had no military objective, are worthy of international condemnation. It is necessary, however, to move the discussion in a pragmatic, nontheoretical direction and put aside consideration of this type of behavior for another time and discussion. For the purposes of creating a political exception and extradition procedure that will successfully operate in an international setting, we must focus our attention on that conduct that has a more individual and direct connection between terrorist and victim, such as a machine gun assault at an airport or the exploding of a civilian airplane in flight. Therefore, it is necessary to distinguish between the violence produced by nations at war or intra-national adversaries on the one hand, and the violence perpetrated by terrorists on the other: "Terrorists are defined by what they do, not by who they are."[13]

The political realignment of Eastern Europe, possibly the most talked-about issue in international politics today, raises thought-provoking questions regarding the proliferation of terrorism. This subject is beyond the scope of this paper, but I will raise at least some of the issues at this point. Will the political and economic transformations in Europe and the strong movements toward reconciliation between East and West, along with the eruption of political and economic insta-

---

11. *Patterns of Global Terrorism* (1988, 1989), Department of State Yearbooks.
12. A plebiscite will be held in June 1991 to determine the wishes of the Puerto Rican population with regard to statehood, independence or enhanced commonwealth status. It is expected that terrorist groups such as the Macheteros will attempt to influence the plebiscite results through the use of violence. *Counter-Terrorism and Security Intelligence* 5, no. 15 (November 1990); see also vol. 4, no. 10 (July 1989).
13. Philip Windsor, book review in *Terrorism and Political Violence* 1, no. 2 (1989), p. 272.

bility within the Warsaw Pact nations, reduce the amount of international terrorism? Will a continued preoccupation, in one form or another, with the "German question" reduce the volume of international terrorism? If there is a united Europe, with the collective will to agree that terrorism is no longer an alternative means of war, will there be a drastic reduction of international terrorism?[14] Will certain countries in North Africa and the Middle East in which terrorism is an active commodity reduce their activities because their prime sponsors are facing additional national and international problems: will they decrease their acts of terrorism and quasi-terrorism as a method of obtaining political dominance over their neighbors and controlling the international flow of oil? Will there be greater cooperation between countries to extradite and identify terrorists? The answer to each of these questions, in my view, is no.[15] Some European countries will continue to fend off the threat of terrorism by permitting safe passage to terrorists or purchasing freedom from this violence by payment for hostages, or by immediate deportation (not extradition or criminal prosecution) of suspected terrorists. For example, although the UK and Czechoslovakia have entered into an agreement to share data relating to terrorism, "Czech security officials said privately it is unlikely all links [to terrorists] have been

---

14. A negative reputation within the international community has not deterred countries such as Libya, Syria, Iraq and Iran from participating in one form or another of international terrorism. Forty-seven nations have agreed to compulsory jurisdiction (but with opting-out provisions) by the International Court of Justice (ICJ). None of the countries named above, including the former Eastern Bloc nations, is a signatory. Joseph Daly, "Is the International Court System Worth the Effort?" *Akron Law Review* 20 (1987), pp. 391, 395.

15. In early 1990, President Assad of Syria informed an invited audience that the Jihad (Holy War) was to continue notwithstanding the USSR's warnings against it. On March 13, 1990, it was widely reported that East Germany had disbanded its security apparatus but that its leader and membership had been "transferred" to the Soviet KGB. In April 1990, it was reported that the French government "paid" for the release of its remaining hostages in the Middle East. In July-August 1990, Iraq's Hussein called for a holy war against the US because of its commitment of US troops in Saudi Arabia. On September 8, 1990 (*The New York Times*, p. 5) the US Department of State warned that "threats of terrorist attacks against the United States had increased sharply since. . .action against Iraq in the Persian Gulf."

broken but they are uneasy about disclosing information to anger terrorist networks."[16] In chapter 2 I will explore whether governments that adhere to the rule of political exception will continue to frustrate the extradition and trial of terrorists.

---

16. *Counter-Terrorism and Security Intelligence* 5, no. 14 (July 1990), p. 5.

1

Terrorism Simplified and the Present Failure of Containment

■ *Definition of Terrorism*

In 1985, a UN General Assembly resolution directed at terrorist activities was adopted by consensus, explicitly and unambiguously condemning as criminal "all acts, methods and practices of terrorism where and by whomever committed."[17] It is interesting and revealing to note in the preamble the General Assembly's obvious difficulty in pinpointing what was encompassed in the term *terrorism*:

> acts . . . which endanger or take innocent human life, jeopardize fundamental freedoms and severely impair the dignity of human beings . . . and covered by the existing conventions relating to various aspects of the problem of terrorism.

Two years later, in 1987, still another resolution condemning terrorism was adopted by the General Assembly, with opposition by the US and Israel. The resolution proposed another convention to be convened to work toward yet another definition for the word *terrorism*. The US and Israel feared that the proponents of the new convention were attempting to formulate a definition that would exclude conduct practiced by the PLO and other such organizations.[18]

---

17. UN General Assembly Res. 40/61 of December 9, 1985 (adopted without vote), para.1.
18. See generally, UN Docs A/C 6/42/sr. 31 (October 29, 1987), pp. 6–7; and A/C 6/42/sr 33 (November 6, 1987), pp. 6–9. See also Antonio Cassese, "The International Community 'Legal' Response to Terrorism," *International Comparative Law Quarterly* 28 (1989), p. 589; and Abraham Sofaer, "Terrorism and the Law," *Foreign Affairs* 64, no. 5 (1986).

It has been said that a conference room with five academics will produce six definitions for the word *terrorism* or *terrorists*. The US government, by itself, has developed many more.[19] *Terrorism* is a word begging to be defined but one that defies a simple, broadly acceptable definition, not merely because there is a constant proliferation of definitions by governments, journalists and academics, among others,[20] but, most importantly, because the acts condemned and declared illegal have their genesis in disparate seeds. The origins of the acts condemned range from international to domestic causes; they arise from clashes of cultural, religious and political systems,[21] as in the case of fringe activists in the animal rights movement throwing dye at fur-coated women in New York, or extremists in the pro-life movement intimidating patients at reproductive health clinics. Thus the great difficulty in attempting to develop one clearly focused and acceptable definition or standard.

What is clear and definable is that a terrorist—even one with the purest of intentions, who seeks respectability—is not a "freedom fighter." This abused and over-utilized cliché arises from a sloppy, imprecise examination of how and where violence is directed. When violence is directed at symbols of a government in power (the military, legislators, diplomats, judges, government and military buildings and installations) by those whose stated aim is its overthrow, then the violence is in one respect a revolution. If the violence, however, is aimed at civilians and civilian property—an airport ticket counter, a school bus filled with children, a tourist bus, an airplane filled with civilians—then the violence is terrorism. A terrorist cannot claim legitimacy as a guerrilla fighting a war of liberation.[22] Guerrilla warfare is a military operation conducted by irregular forces (armed individuals or groups) in enemy-controlled territory or any armed uprising by the people of a nation against

---

19. Note the definition in the US Foreign Intelligence Surveillance Act (50 USCA §1801 et seq.). See Appendix A for several different definitions of the term.
20. Wesleyan University conference on "Terrorism in Context," spring 1989, chaired by Martha Crenshaw. See also Cassese, "The International Community 'Legal' Response to Terrorism."
21. For a description of unrest among minority groups in Eastern Europe, see "Riots Involving Ethnic Rivals," *The New York Times*, February 13, 1990, p. 1.
22. Gerard Chaliand, "Terrorism A Means of Liberation?" *Terrorism and Political Violence* 1, no. 1 (1989).

their "oppressors."[23] My Lai would have been an example of state-sponsored terrorism if the actors had been left unpunished.

It has been argued by Conor Cruise O'Brien that blacks in the southern states of the US in the first half of this century had the right to resort to violence because their access to democracy was "almost nonexistent," their ability to vote denied by violence and fraud, the civil and criminal laws of the nation manipulated and distorted and utilized not to protect them, but employed to curb their freedom of expression and other rights. Under those circumstance, O'Brien concludes, it would be "inappropriate to describe as terrorists those who might use political violence on behalf of such a minority."[24] O'Brien's use of the term *political violence* creates a fuzzy framework within which to approach, define and contain terrorism. In reality, the label *terrorism* should depend upon the target of the "oppressed" and the means used to change the system or deliver the message. If oppressed blacks, as described by O'Brien, had bombed an all-white school bus filled with children, the act would, it is submitted, have been terrorism, notwithstanding the oppression suffered by blacks.

Political ends do not and cannot validate or justify atrocities committed against *a civilian population*. Nor can the argument be that the right exists to employ indiscriminate violence when all other methods to address political, social and economic oppression have failed. The conditions described by O'Brien cannot constitute a license for the use of violence against any accessible target, without regard to the target's participation, or lack thereof, in the alleged wrongdoing suffered by the terrorist. In addition, we cannot accept the argument that one can unilaterally designate a circumscribed geographic area, or even an entire country, as a free fire-zone, i.e., a zone within which weapon fire is expected, and all persons entering the area are presumed to have assumed the risk of

---

23. Jay M. Shafritz et al., *Facts on File Dictionary of Military Science* (New York: Facts on File, 1989). Mao Tse-Tung: "The enemy advances we retreat, the enemy camps we harass; the enemy tires, we attack, the enemy retreats, we pursue."
24. Conor Cruise O'Brien, "Terrorism Under Democratic Conditions," in *Terrorism, Legitimacy, and Power,* ed. Martha Crenshaw (Middletown, CT: Wesleyan University Press, 1983), pp. 94–95.

injury or death.[25] Further, we cannot accept the argument that the commission of a normally condemned criminal act within this designated zone is thereby "politically" permissible, an exception to conduct that would support an extradition order. This syllogism is but another attempt to justify terrorist conduct.

To move toward pragmatic international methods of deterrence and cooperation, terrorism must be viewed in the light of internationally accepted standards of conduct of confrontation, and must be defined by excluding all targets except civilian populations and facilities.

■ *The Need For A Program Of Containment in a Time of Relative Calm*

Through the worldwide media, the dullest of persons is made constantly and acutely aware of the growing sophistication of the methods and the means of destruction available to a terrorist.[26] The worldwide media is also the forum for repeated cries by the vocal that the general public is not being "fully protected" by those whose duty it is to do so, whether it be a particular government or even a particular

---

25. It has been argued that any person, from child to foreign diplomat travelling in any part of Israel, is in a "free fire-zone" and his or her death by a member of recognized terrorist groups is not an act of violence but falls under the political exception doctrine. *In the Matter of the Extradition of Mahmoud Abed Atta a/k/a Mahmoud El-Abed Ahmad*, 706 F. Supp. 1032 (D.C.E.D.N.Y. 1989); *In the Matter of the Petition of Mahmoud El-Abed Ahmad a/k/a Mahmoud Abed Atta v. Wigen, et al*, 726 F. Supp. 389 (D.C.E.D.N.Y. 1989), aff'd 910, F 2d, 1063 (2d Cir. 1990).
26. On February 26, 1990, an NBC TV Channel 4 advertisement in *The New York Times* promoted a special news broadcast examining airport security. The advertisement stated that the area represented by a small black rectangle on the screen was all the space a terrorist needed to blow up an airplane. A feature article in *Newsweek*, August 13, 1990, had the explosive headline: "New Targets For Terror." An article in *Counter-Terrorism and Security Intelligence* 5, no. 2 (January 1990) described four men, three of whom were Irish nationals, who were arrested on January 12, 1990, in West Palm Beach, Florida, attempting to buy US Stinger shoulder-fired anti-aircraft missiles for use against British helicopters, long-range weapons to penetrate British armor and other automatic weapons. It was alleged that the IRA believes that the US is a legitimate place "to hit British interests."

airline.[27] Universally, the "feeling" is one of vulnerability without any means of self-protection or safe haven beyond the door to one's own bedroom.[28] It is interesting to note that terrorism evokes a much more vocal response than does espionage, although both are serious crimes against the state. Acts of terrorism and espionage often call into serious question not only the ability of the government where the criminal act occurred to govern and protect all persons within its territorial boundaries but, after a time, its ability to conduct its own affairs of state. Moreover, an act or successive acts of international terrorism or espionage in one country may have profound and immediate impact beyond the boundaries of the target nation.

Espionage, however, although it is another method to attack the integrity of a government, lacks the public impact and public relations message of a terrorist act.[29] For espionage to be truly successful, the target never learns of the breach in its security or the introduction of misinformation. Consequently, although a country may be placed in jeopardy by an act of espionage, the public, lacking the more immediate impact of violence-generated fear, finds less reason to quickly surrender its social, political and civil rights.

---

27. There is presently pending against Pan Am a civil suit by the relatives of those killed in Scotland, claiming Pan Am's responsibility to protect its passengers against terrorists attacks had been breached. Pan Am in turn claims that the US government knew of the pending attack and withheld the information.

28. Feelings of vulnerability have been increased by incidents of terrorism against vacationing tourists, and by government warnings of possible future incidents. For example, on February 4, 1990, a tour bus with Israeli academics and their families on a holiday was attacked by two masked men near Cairo. Eight tourists were murdered. *The Washington Post*, February 5, 1990, p. 1. The US Department of State announced it was deeply concerned that terrorists "may be" planning an attack on a US target in Western Europe coinciding with the 11th anniversary of Iran's Islamic revolution. *The Wall Street Journal*, February 9, 1990, p. A12. A similar warning was issued in December 1989, citing a high level of activity by the pro-Iranian Shiite Moslem Hezbollah group in Lebanon. While no such attack occurred, the spokesperson for the Department of State said the latest report was based on "direct intelligence" information. It was later reported to this author, by a non-US foreign intelligence officer, that no such terrorist activity had been planned at that time. In September 1990, the US Department of State once again announced the increased risk of a terrorist attack because of the US troop presence in the Persian Gulf region.

29. Espionage is defined as the use of spies to discover the secrets of another nation.

The revelations of the espionage indictment and conviction of John Walker and his accomplices in the United States produced no profound response or outcry from the general public or the media.[30] Although the media repeated the gravity of the harm, there was no editorial clamor claiming negligence or inefficiency by the US military or federal law enforcement agencies or their officers. It is obvious that, privately, the US was not merely embarrassed, it was also compromised in the international intelligence community. Publicly, the "affair" merely seemed to produce a quickly made avenue for a television network to produce a dramatic mini-series. One reason for this public non-response, cynical but clearly supportable, is that Walker and his accomplices, individually and collectively, had no apparent political agenda.[31] The revelations of the Walker case did not create in the public a perception of an immediate personal, dangerous threat. The cynicism lies in the conclusion, as generally reported in the press, that the general public, while not accepting Walker's conduct, understands greed; further rational analysis of the seriousness of the case is thus prevented.

The consequences of a criminal act, therefore, may not necessarily control the national response to the incident. Walker compromised the US national security system, a situation that is initially far more dangerous and, therefore, more fearful than a single terrorist attack that would claim the lives of a few people. But clearly, this should not be interpreted as diminishing the importance of meeting the threat of terrorism. Terrorism affects the very construction and perception of a democratic form of government.

A realistic program of international cooperation and domestic intelligence is acutely necessary, especially because at present the public responses of the United States government and most other countries to international terrorism aimed at its citizens

---

30. *United States v. Walker*, 698 F. Supp. 614 & 103 (D.Md.1985).
31. See generally Gordon Brook-Shepherd, *The Storm Birds* (New York: Weidenfeld & Nicolson, 1989), pp. 40–42. One of the cases discussed here is that of Dr. Alan Nunn May, a British subject who pleaded guilty to providing the Soviet government with highly secret atomic energy information and uranium samples. May claimed that he did not engage in his illegal activity for personal gain, but because he felt that if all parties had the same information "this was a contribution I could make to the safety of mankind."

or interests is usually one of diplomatic posturing and vocal outrage for the media. One need only examine several foreign policy responses of the US to perceived aggression: compare the invasion of tiny Grenada or the invasion of Panama to the long governmental paralysis in response to the Iran hostage ordeal, the hijacking of the *Achille Lauro* with the death of a US citizen, and the fact that US hostages remain captives in West Beirut. Both invasions, Grenada and Panama, must be character-ized as friendly invasions with little chance of failure but with a very good chance of positive media reporting.[32] On the other hand, the US paralysis in the face of the Iran hostage crisis led to the political defeat of the Carter administration in its bid for reelection. The attempted rescue of the hostages was aborted in an Iranian desert in dismal failure. Unlike Grenada and Pan-ama, however, there could be no invasion of Iran, not only because of the likelihood of serious international consequences that would evolve from a prolonged armed intervention, but because of the potential for tremendous loss of lives to the invaders in a politically and socially hostile environment. The number of losses would have been unacceptably high, not only to the operation's military planners, but to a US public that would not have accepted, after the initial excitement generated by the invasion, the ultimate enormity of the consequences.[33]

---

32. The Pentagon announced that it would make it easier for the press to cover military operations, setting out 17 ways to help cover wars. *The New York Times*, March 21, 1990, p. A22. After reading the article, one wonders why or for whom any war is initiated: for the US government's interests or for the press to sell papers "with ready access to the earliest action"? In August 1990, the press complained once again of its limited presence at the time the US troops were gathered for their airlift to Saudi Arabia.

33. The rescue attempt of 52 hostages was aborted in the Iranian desert without contact with any Iranian force, and with eight servicemen killed in the attempted return of the rescue team. "In the end, the combined military and intelligence capabilities of the world's most powerful nation contributed little to the resolution of the hostage crisis." David Martin and John Walcott, *Best Laid Plans* (New York: Harper & Row, 1988). President Carter's secretary of state, Cyrus Vance, was totally convinced that the Iran hostage rescue plan would fail and expressed concern regarding adverse Soviet response to the raid. He resigned his post in protest following the mission's failure. His resignation and the aban-doned US equipment, sensitive documents, and the dead servicemen— all left behind in the desert—were exploited for propaganda purposes by the Iranian government. *Essays on Strategy* (Washington, DC: National Defense University Press, 1985), p. 15. Cf. the US air attack against Libya on the nights of April 14 and 15, 1986. One US aircraft was shot down and its two crewmen were killed. Cf. also the incident of May 1975, when 41

The criminal magnitude of terrorism must be the focal point of not only our domestic responses but also our international commitment to a fully operational plan of cooperation with other nations. This is true whether the violence is a result of a holy war in some far-off country that spills over into the territory of other countries, or is the result of the vengeance of a South American drug lord exploding in Florida or Texas. Cooperation with other nations cannot be merely noted in one more exchange of commitments or in a UN resolution without enforcement procedures. Terrorism is not a passing phenomenon; it has a long history[34] and an even broader spectrum of innovation. It will remain with us in the decades ahead, with changing agendas and targets and with increasing sophistication in the delivery of its destruction.[35]

The necessity for counter-terrorism or surveillance (in its purest sense and not as a tool of repression and terrorism) can run directly counter to the imperatives of due process and the protection of an individual's civil and social rights.[36] But whether a terrorist act constitutes political, noncriminal behavior rather than criminal behavior is an interesting exercise for those who seek the etiology of such conduct or for those who hope to reduce or eliminate the impact of the offense in determining the guilt or innocence of a defendant in the dock. It is not the intent of this paper to suggest that governments ignore the root of the problems that may cause the violence. That is another issue. What cannot be forgotten (as most often is the case) is that a violent offense executed by any person or group as a means of communicating a political, racial, social or economic statement or outrage cannot be examined within an equation that omits the victim. In most instances of a terrorist strike, the victim has no stake in the conditions complained of by the terrorist—thus the use of the term "random violence."[37]

Marines were killed trying to rescue the 39 crewmen of the US merchant ship *Mayaguez*, which had been seized by the Cambodian government.

34. "One of the earliest known examples of terrorist movements is the sicarii, a highly organized religious sect in the Zealot struggle in Palestine in AD 66–73." Walter Laqueur, *Age of Terrorism*, p. 12.
35. See Robert Kupperman and Jeff Kamen, *Final Warning* (New York: Doubleday, 1989).
36. See Crelinsten, "Terrorism, Counter-Terrorism and Democracy."
37. "Generally speaking, a valid criterion is whether or not there is anything to connect the victim directly or indirectly with the aims or objectives pursued by the offenders and with the countries in the conflict area or

And while it is also a truism that dissent is an integral element of any open government, the right to dissent has bounds that cannot withstand illegal behavior that culminates in the loss of civilian life or civilian property. Society has not accepted that immediate and personal fear of death from an unseen enemy can be a defense to the atrocities of My Lai. Similarly, it should not permit a terrorist to unilaterally define a free fire-zone to excuse the murder of civilians. On balance, "while the (US) Constitution protects against invasions of an individual's rights, it is not a suicide pact."[38] The same premise is true for all other nations.

Yehezkel Dror, reviewing the challenges to a democracy by terrorism, has developed principal and secondary forms of terrorism, four of them having relevance to this paper.[39]

1. Imported terrorism by and on behalf of aliens.
2. Transient terrorism by aliens against aliens on the territory of a democracy.
3. Terrorism against nongovernment targets within a democracy.
4. Extraterritorial terrorism against external representatives of symbols of a democracy.

A fifth category could be added, or it may be argued that it falls under the first: Transient terrorism by aliens on the territory of a democracy against nongovernment symbols to affect the host government's response. These forms of terrorism are but a small handful of problems law enforcement officials must confront, with a constant flow of new variations, emerging causes, changing motives, and profiles.[40] This creates part of the difficulty in facing this constant threat. As previously noted, terrorism cannot be eradicated, but the number and severity of successful incidents can be reduced significantly through legitimate international cooperation, utilizing non-revengeful, non-repressive counter-terrorism measures whose

---

with the relevant political situation." "Guide for Combating International Terrorism," I.C.P.O.-Interpol, Resolution no. AGN/53/RES/7. See also Crelinsten, "Terrorism, Counter-Terrorism and Democracy," fn 57.

38. Justice Arthur J. Goldberg delivering the opinion of the court in *Kennedy v. Martinez-Mendosa*, 372 U.S.144, 160 (1962).
39. Yehezkel Dror, "Challenge to the Democratic Capacity to Govern," in *Terrorism, Legitimacy and Power*, ed. Chrenshaw.
40. For example, on August 12, 1990, a Swiss hostage was released in Lebanon by a terrorist group not before identified.

aim is containment.[41] The aim of containment, if not to reduce the number of incidents, is to reduce those incidents that produce severe casualties, such as Pan Am 103.

■ *The Present Failure of Containment Programs*

The human cry demanding an armed intervention—reflected in the media in response to terrorist events—is predictable and most often predicated on insufficient information or analysis. If such was the scenario when, as in the Iranian hostage crises, the participants were known and the cry for help by the victims was heartrending to a nation,[42] what can be the response when the composition of the terrorist group claiming responsibility is possibly but not absolutely clear?

Terrorism and terrorist groups are either self-sustaining or part of the very fabric of a state support system and involvement, which renders containment all the more difficult. Robert Kupperman describes the former as "self-sustaining organisms" that operate without significant involvement of a particular state:

> They may move from state to state or operate from some jurisdictional no-man's land, such as portions of Lebanon. If they operate from a single state, state officials may not know of them or may actually oppose them but be unable to deal with them effectively.[43]

Between self-sustaining and state-sponsored terrorism (where the state recruits, directs, finances and incites terrorist activity) there is a middle ground, where support takes on varying forms: sanctuary, tolerance of presence, financial sup-

---

41. Steven Metz, "An American Strategy for Low-Intensive Conflict," *Strategic Review* 17 (Fall 1989). Containment makes use of counter-terrorism measures to both deter terrorism and make the execution of a terrorist attack more difficult.

42. With the beginning of the Iranian hostage crisis, the American Broadcast Company began a nightly network broadcast covering each day's events as they pertained to the hostages. The commentator was an "almost" unknown, Ted Koppel. The program was a psychological outlet for the US public, which had no other way to express its national outrage and frustration at the inaction of its own government.

43. Robert Kupperman, "Terror, the Strategic Tool: Response and Control," *Annals of Political Science* 436 (1982), pp. 32–33.

port, training, arms, intelligence, etc.[44] What can be the government's response when the terrorist group is partially identifiable but the members are dispersed and hidden within an innocent, sometimes complacent, sometimes enforced environment? The Romanian scholar Daniel Daianu said that in Bucharest after the execution of Ceausescu, the security forces continued their sniping with automatic weapons from apartment building complexes in order to create panic and unrest. He then posed the dilemma: What was the army to do? Destroy an entire block of apartment buildings to get half a handful of snipers?[45]

The US Department of State claims a comprehensive four-pronged strategy to respond to the problems of international terrorism.[46] The first of its counter-terrorism policies is that there are to be no concessions, payments of ransom, release of convicted terrorists or changes in stated policy to accommodate terrorist demands.[47] The second calls for retaliation carried out so that a state sponsor of terrorism would suffer in some definable and identifiable physical or psychological way; the US has the additional option of imposing political, economic and diplomatic sanctions.[48] An obvious example of this ap-

---

44. Kenneth Abbott, "Economic Sanctions and International Terrorism," *Vanderbilt Journal of Transnational Law* 20 (1987), p. 289.
45. Jonathan P. Bach, "Daniel Daianu on the Current Political and Economic Situation in Romania," Institute for East-West Security Studies Meeting Report, January 23, 1990.
46. *Patterns of Global Terrorism*, 1988, Department of State Yearbook.
47. Was the Iran-Contra affair an aberration or was it the first element of US counter-terrorism policy not expected to be observed? In April and May of 1990, it was hinted by President Bush that there was some indirect contact with those holding the US hostages. An April 8, 1990, announcement by the French government of the release of a French citizen held hostage in the Middle East after "successful negotiations" between the French government and Qaddafi makes it likely to assume that the French government agreed to substantial financial considerations to Libya.
48. "Economic Measures Against Libya," *International Legal Materials* 25 (1986), p. 173; *Christian Science Monitor*, December 29, 1988, p. 3. L. Paul Bremmer III, the United States Ambassador-at-Large for Counter-Terrorism, noted that the US had sufficient success in closing down the operation of several terrorist groups with quiet diplomacy by approaching a country with information regarding the activities of a group and saying: "We (the US) are concerned about this terrorist-related activity that your government may not be aware of." In "most" cases, Bremmer asserted, the government reacted positively to the information. See also L. Paul

proach offered by the Office of the Ambassador-at-Large for Counter-terrorism was the 1986 bombing raid of Libya.[49]

The third policy calls for the US government to protect US citizens abroad and to cooperate with friendly nations and allies in identifying, tracking, apprehending, prosecuting and punishing terrorists "by using the rule of law." Yet Abul Abbas and his associates in the planning and execution of the hijacking and murder of a US citizen aboard the *Achille Lauro* were in the custody first of the Egyptian and then the Italian governments. Abbas and his immediate lieutenant were never prosecuted, but were spirited out of Egypt and allowed to flee Italy to a safe haven in Yugoslavia.[50]

The last prong of the department's anti-terrorism approach is its Training Assistance Program, which provides instruction in anti-terrorism techniques for law enforcement officials around the world. It is important to note that the US Department of State is but one branch of this government that has a program of intelligence-gathering in the area of counter-terrorism. Notwithstanding all these developed techniques and policies, Pan Am 103 was destroyed in the air over Lockerbie on December 21, 1988, with a loss of 259 lives, including 189 US citizens and 11 others on the ground.[51]

Although there may be exceptions created by the hostilities initiated by Iraq and the troops of several nations stationed

---

Bremmer III, "Practical Measures of Dealing with Terrorism," *US Department of State Bulletin*, March 1987.

49. *Patterns of Global Terrorism*, 1988, Department of State Yearbook. See also Greenwood, "International Law and The United States Operation Against Libya."

50. See generally Martin and Walcott, *Best Laid Plans*, in particular the chapter describing the *Achille Lauro* affair and the Italian government's refusal to hold the hijackers. "Craxi was more interested in preserving his good relation with the PLO and with Egypt than he was in arresting Abbas, whose apprehension might trigger terrorist attacks against Italy" (p. 255). "Egypt's Mubarak was furious. . .(but) time and $2 billion a year in aid (from the US) was (to) salve (his) wounds" (p. 257).

51. "The German Connection," *The New York Times*, March 18, 1990. The premise of the article is that the West Germans had all the persons involved in the planning and execution of the attack on Pan Am 103 in custody prior to the December crash, but German intelligence and security personnel and their judiciary system failed to fully or carefully investigate the facts or connections to other evidence or to fully press the investigation of the terrorists' activities. The German intelligence community, it is claimed by the authors, then attempted to cover up their failures.

in Saudi Arabia, terrorism continues to direct most of its violence toward the least protected targets: tourists and nonmilitary, nongovernmental business.[52] This creates not only the perception of the necessity for an individual to take charge of his or her personal safety in those instances where responsibility was formerly assumed by carriers or nations, but it creates additional psychological pressure.

In light of the general ineffectiveness internationally in responding to terrorism, how would any one nation react to the following scenarios had they taken place within their jurisdiction? First scenario: A Fourth of July in the US. A massive fireworks display commences. Bombs previously placed in areas likely to contain thousands of onlookers start to explode in sequence, with massively lethal results. Stunned disbelief is followed by telephone calls with multiple parties claiming responsibility. What then? Second scenario: On a deserted strip of highway, a tour bus is forced to the side of the road and two masked terrorists spray the bus with automatic weapon fire and hand grenades. What then?

In response to the multiple sources of terrorism, there has been a proliferation of multilateral anti-terrorism conventions that require signatory states to take custody of an accused person and proceed either with a criminal trial or extradition. The failure of those types of conventions or the rule of *aut dedere, aut judicare* (literally, "either surrender or prosecute"), as presently constituted, is more than obvious upon a cursory reading of the facts in either the *Achille Lauro* incident in October 1984 or the "German connection" in the downing of Pan Am 103 in December 1988.[53] Both of these will be discussed in detail in chapter 2.

---

52. In early 1990, a new threat emerged against airlines and state-controlled airlines. The "Islamic Holy War for the Liberation of Palestine," a militant Muslim group in Lebanon, threatened to attack airlines and airports that help transport the new wave of Jewish settlers to Israel. *The New York Times*, March 22, 1990, p. A18. In addition, the US troop presence in the Iraq-Saudi war prompted intelligence officials to announce in mid-August (*The New York Times*, August 18, 1990, p. 5) that, although it "is not going to be an easy task" to attack US military and diplomatic installations, "more potential targets arrive (t)here every day." In September, the Department of State announced that the threat of terrorist attacks against the US "has increased sharply" in all regions (*The New York Times*, September 8, 1990, p. 5).
53. Steven Emerson and Brian Duffy, "Pan Am 103: The German Connection," *The New York Times Magazine*, March 18, 1990, p. 28.

■ Meeting the Continuing Threat to Containment

A. Extradition

Although there is consensus and recognition by many governments, with varying degrees of commitment, of the need to develop and enhance sources and means of intelligence, the terrorist has neither the lack of ingenuity nor failure of determination that appears to be exhibited by many nations. Containment has its obvious costs beyond merely those involved in economic appropriations for personnel and equipment to meet the ongoing challenge. As discussed in this paper, containment requires a program that would permit a narrowly defined area of extended domestic electronic surveillance of certain persons (as discussed in chapter 3), as well as a redefinition of the political exception defense. This defense permits a defendant to fight extradition by alleging that

1. his or her act of violence was "political" or executed in a political context;
2. he or she will not receive a fair or adequate trial in the requesting state; and
3. conditions of imprisonment in the requesting state are inhumane.

The redefining of the political exception process[54] would be the first step toward a more comprehensive plan that encompasses both that process and an international extradition procedure under the jurisdiction of the International Court of Justice (ICJ).[55] The latter program would require a two-pronged ap-

---

54. On the political exception rule, see generally the opinions of Judge Korman and Judge Weinstein in the matter involving Mahmoud Abed Atta a/k/a Mahmoud El-Abed Ahmad. *Matter of Extradition of Atta,* 706 F.Supp. 1032 (E.D.N.Y. 1989) and *Ahmad v. Wigen,* 726 F.Supp. 389 (E.D.N.Y. 1989).

55. The International Court of Justice (ICJ) is a large and, at times, unwieldy body of 15 judges, no two of whom may be nationals of the same state. They are elected by both the UN General Assembly and the Security Council. Although there is no formal rule allocating seats on the bench, in practice, each of the permanent members of the Security Council is voted one seat. A nation need not accept the court's jurisdiction without reservation. As other nations have done, the United States, when prompted by a particular case, has given notice of its decision to terminate acceptance of jurisdiction. The ICJ is considered an international court of "universal character". There are a number of other permanent but regional international courts such as the Court of Justice of the

proach: the first is the unconditional commitment by all members of the United Nations to the jurisdiction of the ICJ in a limited type of extradition proceeding. The second is the agreement that all nations will redefine the scope and use of political barriers to limit the availability of extradition.

A coercive approach to extradition will require nations to relinquish unconditionally a portion of their sovereign rights to the ICJ. Terrorists do understand and appreciate the law, when they know there is a legal escape hatch;[56] what they must be made aware of, in a direct and unambiguous manner, is the universal commitment that acts of violence will be deemed illegal if aimed at a civilian population or facility.[57] The proposal suggested in this paper recognizes sovereign-international prerogatives, but offers three reasons in support of relinquishing those powers:

1. It would relieve the pressures inherent in bilateral and narrow multilateral treaties of extradition. If initially all the major players were to agree openly to this proposal, one reason for denying extradition or ignoring a treaty, namely fear of retaliation by the terrorist group that supports the person who is to be extradited, would be reduced. The combined intelligence and resources of all the signatories would then be available in opposition to a terrorist group or its sponsor. There is, therefore, a safety-in-numbers incentive with mutual cooperation.

2. There is greater political pressure to comply when there are multiple parties to an agreement.

3. Finally, there is the element of expectations. If one party adheres to a multiparty agreement, it is expected others will also. If one party fulfills its obligation to extradite an offender, then its own demand for extradition will be more readily acknowledged, when it becomes a demanding state.

European Communities (the judicial organ of the European Common Market), the European Court of Human Rights (the judicial organ of the European Convention for the Protection of Human Rights), the Benelux Court of Justice (whose function is to ensure "uniformity in the interpretation" of Benelux treaties whose purpose is to advance the objectives of the Union), and the Inter-American Court of Human Rights, whose seat is in San Jose, Costa Rica.

56. Guilt or innocence was ignored, and a protracted and technically intricate procedural defense was employed by the attorneys to provide the basis for a dismissal of an indictment against a claimed terrorist who was caught with several bombs. US v. Kikumura, Crime No.88–166 (D.N.J.).

57. On distinguishing these acts from sabotage, see 18 USCA §2151 et seq.

B. Political Exception Rule

Courts and commentators generally view political offenses or crimes as one of two types. The first type are those offenses with little if any violence attached to the act, and if there is violence its object is rarely a civilian population. This type of offense is considered directly or purely political: examples are treason, prohibited speech and flag burning. In addition, this type of offense is thought of as peaceful political activity and as a means for individuals to obtain political change. Consequently, the pure or direct political act does not generally form a basis for extradition.

The second type of offense finds its genesis in a common criminal act, but with the claim by the defendant that his or her act was either politically motivated or was committed in a political context and, therefore, is not an extraditable crime but a political statement.[58] It is within this category that difficulties arise.

In the development of the political exception the initial criterion is the "incidence test"—the exception is a shield against extradition if the criminal act committed by the petitioner was "incidental to or formed a part of a political disturbance."[59] In other words, the act that forms the basis of a defense against extradition must have occurred during or incidental to or in aid of a severe political revolt, insurrection, civil war, rebellion or revolution.

As part of the extradition proposal, and as a first step toward the international control of extradition in cases of terrorism, nations must limit the use and scope of the political exception rule. According to the concept *aut dedere aut judicare*, a state must either prosecute an offender found within its territory or extradite the person to a demanding state. As noted, it has not worked. The extradition procedure proposed under the neutral jurisdiction of the ICJ and the limiting of the political exception rule are not mutually exclusive. As will be proposed and discussed in chapter 2, under strict, universally accepted rules of neutral procedure, evidence, and disclosures by requesting nations, certain terrorists *must* be extradited without reference to national political exception rules or pol-

---

58. Both types of offense are discussed in *Ahmad v. Wigen*, 726 F. Supp. 389,401 (E.D.N.Y. 1989).
59. *In re Castioni*, 1 Q.B. 149, 166 (1890).

icy.[60] Defendants with citizenship ties to the requested nation should be provided additional protection by the country of citizenship with reference to the political exception rule, but only if those killed were not civilians.[61]

C. Electronic Surveillance

What must be accepted as a given in any discussion of counter-terrorism is that available, accurate, and timely intelligence is rarely available to the extent necessary to fully protect a target or foil a terrorist attack.[62] Collecting intelligence on terrorist groups is an enormous challenge faced by the FBI, CIA, National Security Agency, and other US and foreign intelligence organizations.[63]

How often does an intelligence analyst truly understand all the bits and pieces of information as they are gathered? How often is there a completed picture? The analysts must make leaps of assumption. Prior to Yu Kikumura's arrest in April 1988, he traveled about the US purchasing the material necessary to make several bombs. His arrest was not accomplished through any sophisticated use of an intelligence apparatus or network of foreign or domestic intelligence gathering, but through pure happenstance and luck when a New Jersey state trooper "felt" the defendant's behavior suspicious.[64] This dem-

---

60. Extradition and political exception requirements and neutral procedures would be those adopted by the ICJ, utilizing accepted norms of conduct.
61. The US has refused to extradite to the UK a defendant accused of killing a noncivilian, although he remains in custody. *In re Doherty*, 599 F. Supp.270 (S.D.N.Y.1984).
62. An intelligence gap was complained of by the authorities after the IRA assassination of British lawmaker Ian Gow in 1990, even though the police had discovered his name on an Irish Republican Army "hit list" in 1988. "New Targets for Terrorism," *Newsweek*, August 13, 1990, p. 42.
63. "Terrorism poses substantial difficulties for primary deterrence. First because of their tactics, terrorists are often hard to identify and apprehend." Kenneth Abbott, "Economic Sanctions and International Terrorism." See generally, L. Paul Bremmer III, "Practical Measures of Dealing with Terrorism."
64. When asked why he decided to investigate Kikumura's presence in a New Jersey parking lot, the arresting state trooper replied that he had a "gut" reaction. Had the arrest not taken place, in all likelihood his actions would have resulted in several successful international terrorist attacks in the US. In another situation, when asked why an Israeli intelligence officer decided to detain a person at a European airport, who as it turned out was attempting to blow up an El Al flight, the intelligence officer

25

onstrates the great difficulty of interdiction, let alone the weakness of the notion of initial intelligence that points to an "act of violence to take place *some time in the future*."[65]

The second method of containment, as discussed in chapter 3 of this paper, is extended electronic surveillance of a limited classification of persons who can be classified as "sleepers." Briefly, a sleeper is a person who is introduced into the US for the sole purpose of being called upon at some future, indeterminate date to participate with others or alone to produce a violent, non-sabotage incident. The initial problem with electronic surveillance, as either an intelligence or counter-terrorism tool, is to safeguard and protect the constitutional rights of a target and those in contact with the target. With electronic surveillance, there is clearly an invasion of a person's right to privacy and an unlawful government surveillance if undertaken prior to a conspiracy to commit or to the actual commission of an illegal act.[66] A narrow exception must be created to meet the nature and method of a sleeper's activities. Where, by reason of intelligence gathering and profile (notwithstanding the determination that the intelligence gathered falls short of the usual standards for permitting electronic surveillance),[67] the strong possibility exists that the target may be a sleeper, who will engage in future criminal activity, with "terrorism" as his or her goal, then extended electronic surveillance would be permitted pursuant to the procedures proposed in this paper. The electronic surveillance method proposed balances a government's obligation to protect the entire population within its borders with independent and extensive safeguards to protect the individual's right to be free of unwarranted surveillance.

---

replied simply to this writer: "There was something that did not fit together about this man."

65. Martha Crenshaw, "The Causes of Terrorism," *Comparative Politics,* July 13, 1981, pp. 379–399. (emphases added in text). See also Crelinsten, "Terrorism, Counter-Terrorism and Democracy"; also *Newsweek*, August, 13, 1990, p. 42.

66. The US Foreign Intelligence Surveillance Act, as interpreted by the federal courts, distinguishes between electronic surveillance as a method of collecting information concerning the security of the US and evidence collected for criminal prosecution. *US v. Megahey*, 553 F. Supp. 1180, aff'd. 729 F.2d 1144 (D.C.N.Y. 1982); *Matter of Kevork*, 634 F. Supp. 1015 (C.D. Ca. 1985).

67. The usual standard is that the evidence submitted on a wiretap application to a court must present sufficient evidence that there is more reason than not to believe that a crime is about to take place or has taken place.

2

Political Considerations and International Extradition

■ *Two Case Studies*

In many nations with integrated systems of governance and extensive use of technocrats to operate the daily mechanism of government, the violent elimination of an elected leader will not, in all likelihood, signal the demise of a duly installed administration. Terrorists have learned to understand this phenomenon, and, therefore, have altered their approach to random violence aimed at civilians and civilian targets.

The following two classic cases are examples that highlight the faults in the international extradition system as it is presently constituted. Each case study is symptomatic of the serious international legal and political problems that arise when a terrorist is "found" within one jurisdiction and seeks to prevent international extradition to the site of the crime or to the nation that claims the breach of its criminal statutes. The first is a matter just concluded in the federal courts of the United States. The second occurred in Egypt and Italy. In the first example, the terrorist claims, among other defenses, that his act of violence was a political statement and that, therefore, he is relieved of all criminal liability by the state demanding his extradition. The second example is more political in nature—a nation, finding an alleged terrorist within its territory, frustrates the extradition process out of fear of triggering a continuing retaliation from the terrorist's sponsor, by permitting or even facilitating the immediate transfer (the more appropriate word is escape) of the terrorist to a friendly, harboring country.

The first case occurred in April 1986. Three men who had

previously studied the time schedule of a suburban bus company and the terrain its buses traveled waited until dark on a Saturday evening, until a lone bus with three passengers and a driver approached a quiet intersection. The three men first hurled Molotov cocktails at the bus, then strafed the vehicle with automatic weapon fire. The civilian bus driver was fatally wounded, another passenger was struck by shrapnel and rounds from a submachine gun, and the two remaining passengers escaped injury. The entire incident occurred in Israel; all the persons on the bus were Israeli citizens.

The Abu Nidal organization immediately claimed responsibility for the attack. Two of the three assailants were captured, and a third escaped. In 1987 Israel learned that the escaped assailant, Mahmoud Abed Atta, also known as Mahmoud El-Abed Ahmad, was living in Venezuela. Ahmad had been implicated by his confederates after their capture. Venezuelan authorities placed Ahmad on a flight to the United States, because, among other reasons immaterial to this discussion, he was a naturalized US citizen. Fourteen months after the attack, Israel formally requested that the United States extradite Ahmad.[68] More than three years passed before the US federal court system permitted his extradition so that he could be brought to trial in Israel, on, among other charges, murder and attempted murder, both of which were violations of various sections of the Israeli penal law.

The second case occurred in October 1984, when four armed men took control of a vessel with a crew of 344 and 97 passengers. The crime at that moment was the hijacking of an Italian ship—the *Achille Lauro*—off the coast of Egypt, which was, consequently, a crime under Italian law. The hijackers demanded the release of 50 Palestinians (who had been convicted of such crimes as murder) being held in Israeli prisons. By the end of the second day of the hijacking, the terrorists murdered a passenger from the United States and threw his body overboard. The leader of the four terrorists on board the vessel, Abul Abbas, remained in ship-to-shore radio communi-

---

68. *In the Matter of the Extradition of Mahmoud Abed Atta, a/k/a/ Mahmoud El-Abed Ahmad*, 706 F. Supp. 1032 (E.D.N.Y. 1989); *In the Matter of the Petition of Mahmoud El-Abed Ahmad a/k/a/ Mahmoud Abed Atta v. George Wigen, as Warden of Metropolitan Correction Center of the Federal Bureau of Prisons, et al*, 726 F. Supp. 389 (E.D.N.Y. 1989), Affd. 910 F. 2d 1063 (2d. Cir. 1990).

cation with his men and gave them directions to underline the "objectives" of their attack. At the same time, because the attack had gone "sour," the PLO stepped in posing as a disinterested broker, and Abbas (not yet identified in his role in the hijacking) was nominated by Arafat to "negotiate" with the terrorists holding the hostages. When the vessel entered an Egyptian port, the four terrorists were placed aboard a tugboat and taken ashore. Within 30 minutes, the world knew that a US citizen had been killed in the hijacking.

Notwithstanding these events, the Egyptian government informed the world press that, pursuant to the terms of the hostage negotiations, but prior to learning of the fate of the US traveler, the terrorists had left Egypt. In truth, the terrorists had been taken ashore and they were still in Egypt with Abbas. The Egyptian government then attempted to fly the terrorists out of the country to a destination of their choice. After being airborne for a period of time, the plane was intercepted by two US fighter jets that forcibly escorted the Egyptian airplane to Italy.[69] Also on board the airplane were Abbas and a companion who was identified as the second-ranking person in the PLO's Cairo office. At this point, it was determined by intelligence sources that Abbas had taken his orders from the inception of the hijacking from Arafat and the PLO.

The Italian government prevented US representatives from boarding the Egyptian aircraft or arresting the four hijackers and Abbas. Five days after the hijacking, the Italian government removed the four terrorists from the Egyptian airplane and arrested them after they had been positively identified by some of the passengers from the *Lauro*. Abbas and his companion were permitted to remain on board the plane by the Italian government. Seven days after the hijacking, the Italian government was presented with a provisional US arrest warrant seeking the extradition of Abbas. Although the treaty of extra-

---

69. It is claimed by the US authorities that the illegal intrusion into a foreign country would not be a violation of the defendant's constitutional rights in the US. It is interesting to note, however, the Mexican government's reaction: it claimed that a Mexican citizen "had been captured" in Mexico by bounty hunters responding to a reward offered by the United States. *The New York Times*, April 20, 1990, p. 1. In a non-terrorism context, Canadian authorities have arrested a number of US bounty hunters who had sought to capture persons who were subjects of US court proceedings.

dition between the United States and Italy provided for the holding of a suspect up to 45 days, the Italian government alleged that *"under Italian law"* the factual and substantive allegations of the US request were insufficient. That very day Abbas and his PLO companion were transferred to a Yugoslav airline and flown to Belgrade, where they took refuge in the PLO embassy in that city.

What occurred in both case studies was that a state breached its responsibility to maintain its reputation within the international community as neither a state sponsor nor state supporter of terrorism. The extradition process was corrupted indirectly in the US case and directly by the governments of Egypt and Italy. In the first example, the political exception rule, as a defense to the terms of a bilateral treaty of extradition, was distorted by permitting its manipulative use by Ahmad through three hearings. In the *Achille Lauro* incident, a bilateral treaty was virtually ignored.

■ *Political Considerations and Extradition*

A United Nations declaration imposes a duty upon each state to refrain from permitting its territory or resources to be utilized for the violent overthrow of the regime of another state.[70] It is claimed by some that it is unclear whether harboring a terrorist before or after a terrorist attack that occurs outside a state's territory would violate the duty and obligation contained in the declaration.[71] This approach, it is submitted, not only perverts the declaration's meaning, but has no rational or legal basis.

Extradition treaties are, in the simplest terms, contracts or agreements where both (or all) parties have the same expecta-

---

70. Declaration on Principles of International Law Concerning Friendly Relations and Cooperation Among States in Accordance with the Charter of the United Nations, October 24, 1970, G.A.Res. 2625, 25 U.N. GAOR Supp (No. 28) at 121 U.N. Doc. A/8028 (1971) reprinted in 9 I.L.M. 1292; reaffirmed in the Tokyo Economic Summit Statement on Terrorism, May 5, 1986 reprinted in *Department of State Bulletin* (July 1986), p. 5. (See Appendix B). Cf. US extraterritorial jurisdiction over terrorist acts abroad against US nationals. Federal Code, Chapter 113A.
71. Roda Mushkat, "When War May Justifiably Be Waged"; Christopher Greenwood, "International Law and the United States Air Operation Against Libya."

tion. In traditional extradition proceedings, one country forwards a formal request pursuant to the terms of their treaty for the production of a person to stand trial in the requesting nation. The requested nation then complies with the request, the expectation being that those persons accused of a crime will be returned to the site of the alleged criminal act. If the crime was committed against a citizen (or property) of a nation, but not within that nation's territory, the defendant would be sent to the country of the victim's citizenship. The rationale is that a nation suffers an injury when one of its citizens is attacked within or outside its own territory, and, therefore, has the right and obligation to extract the criminal penalty due.[72]

The multiple proceedings and appeal that evolved in the *Ahmad* case are excellent examples of the serious problems facing requesting nations seeking extradition for the purposes of criminal prosecution. The judicial process in the US permitted Ahmad three separate evidentiary hearings in the Federal District Court (before three different judges) to determine the facts and issues underlying his political exception defense. He then appealed the denial of his defense and the extradition order of the District Court judges to the United States Court of Appeals. Although the appellate court affirmed his extradition to Israel, the entire judicial process consumed more than three years of the federal courts' time and attention from the moment the Israeli government requested his extradition to the time of the Court of Appeals decision. The treaty between the United States and Israel states that extradition will be unavailable when "the offense is regarded by the *requested* party [in the Ahmad case, this would be the United States; Israel would be the *requesting* party] as one of a political character." Not surprisingly, the term *political* is not fully defined in the treaty.[73] In determining whether Ahmad's conduct was political, the United States federal courts looked to the laws of their own country in determining its scope and meaning.[74] This approach has positive and negative implications. Why should the US determine

---

72. The US claims jurisdiction over a terrorist act against US nationals even when committed outside the territorial sovereignty of the country. 18 U.S.C.A § 2331.
73. Note the United States-United Kingdom 1985 extradition treaty taking greater care to define such words as "political." See Appendix B.
74. *Eain v. Wilkes*, 641 F.2d 504, 508,512 (7th Cir.), cert. denied, 454 U.S. 894, 102 S. Ct.390, 70 L.Ed.2d 208 (1981).

the political implications of an act committed in another sovereign nation? On the other hand, this approach will protect defendants from the consequences of attempting to overthrow a repressive state.

Although the executive branch of the United States has the ultimate authority to prevent extradition, how the political exception rule will be applied initially in a particular matter is for the federal courts to determine. Their approach to this problem has traveled beyond the mere incidence test.

It is the courts, in the first instance, that are to define a political act sufficient to meet the incidence test. Requiring a frame of reference, the courts may turn to (among other measuring devices) the foreign policy views of the executive branch of their government.[75] So long as the views of the Department of State do not represent a radical departure from acceptable international norms, the courts will give great weight to its determination in deciding whether a particular offense falls within the political exception rule. The courts are not to ignore current international policy toward the containment of terrorism. Indeed, the Council of Europe specifically excludes in its Convention on Terrorism the political exception defense as an option in treaties between members of the Council.[76]

The validity of the political exception defense has a sound place in international law, since it permits the overthrow of intolerable regimes or governments, but it should not be activated by any member of the international community when the violence results in the injury or death of civilians or those who are not by logical deduction part of or an extension to a military or paramilitary force. The courts of the United States have not uniformly approached the issue of defining or distinguishing the various targets of terrorism, the realities of modern terrorism, or the court's role in the inquiry. In addition, nations have not reached a consensus as to the role of this or similar policies and defenses.

In 1981, it was determined by a United States federal court that a Palestine Liberation Organization member, who had been accused of detonating a bomb in a public square that

---

75. *Ahmad v. Wigen*, 726 F. Supp. 389, 403 (E.D.N.Y 1989).
76. European Convention on the Suppression of Terrorism, arts. 1 & 2, *European Year Book* 25 (1977), pp. 289–90; *International Legal Materials* 15 (1976), pp. 1272–73. See Appendix B.

killed two and injured 36 civilians, could not escape extradition by claiming political exception. The court concluded that the law is not "utterly absurd," nor does it "afford immunity to those who commit atrocities for political ends," nor was it meant to protect "indiscriminate bombing of a civilian populace ... even when the larger political objective ... (is) to eliminate the civilian population of a country."[77] Yet, another federal appellate court of equal standing turned a blind eye toward humanity and held that: "We believe the tactics that are used in ... political internal struggles are simply irrelevant to the question of whether the political offense exception is applicable."[78] In effect, the second court was permitting the licensing of an atrocity if it is undertaken to further a political purpose; the court found no justification in distinguishing between military and civilian targets. "All that the courts would do is determine whether the conduct is related to or connected with the insurgent activity." Presently there is a "lack of uniformity in US court decisions" with the "near total absence of objective legal standards on this issue."[79]

This brings us to the crux of the issue and the international dilemma created by the political exception defense. The justifications that Ahmad claimed for his acts were that his victims lacked political legitimacy, that the victims were present in a free fire-zone (which he created by implication) so that *anyone* present in the area of attack had entirely assumed the risk of being killed, and that "none of the settlers, be they man, woman or child, can legitimately lay claim to civilian status." None of Ahmad's claims is internationally acceptable. No nation, let alone a court, has the right to permit or license an atrocity against a *civilian* population. Therefore, for all nations, extradition becomes the most important tool to contain terrorism. Consequently, international political posturing and domestic predisposition to "causes" must be removed from the process of determining the criteria and use of the political exception defense and the elements of extradition.[80]

---

77. *Eain v. Wilkes* 614 F.2d 504 (7th Cir. 1981).
78. *Quinn v. Robinson*, 783 F.2d, 776, 804–05, cert. denied, 479 U.S. 882, 107 S. Ct. 271 (1986).
79. *Matter of Extradition of Pazienz*, 619 F. Supp. 611. 619 (D.C.N.Y.1985).
80. In the summer of 1988, a US-Soviet task force to prevent terrorism met to agree upon goals to prevent, limit and punish acts of terrorism. What was agreed upon contained material stumbling blocks to meaningful judicial

■ The Need for One Set of Extradition Criteria

It is not the intention of this paper to argue for the elimination of the political exception rule as a historical, valid and humanitarian defense exercised in pursuit of legitimate change. Therein lies part of the dilemma: can nations define "legitimate change" while at the same time preventing harsh or dictatorial governments from arbitrarily seeking extradition of opponents? The proposed program to overcome this problem is a universal extradition process. Proposed is a two-step political exception rule as a preliminary move toward control of the entire process, which will utilize internationally agreed standards of political exception and extradition, to be ultimately applied by the neutral International Court of Justice. What is not suggested is the reconsideration of an international criminal court for the trial of terrorists.

The ICJ in its proposed role is not to be viewed as an international criminal court, as was first envisioned 70 years ago. Briefly, the history of the ICJ begins in June-July 1920, in the new Peace Palace at the Hague, when an advisory committee of jurists met to draft a statute for a Permanent Court of International Justice. The committee of jurists proposed the establishment of a High Court of International Justice "to try crimes against international public order and the universal law of nations."[81]

The problems that prevented its adoption were the inability of nations to agree to the indispensable definitions needed for various offenses, and the necessity of agreement by all states to extradite accused persons to an international court for trial. The committee of jurists facing these two problems simply passed a "resolution in the form of a wish (*voeux*)" that such a court be considered. There was much activity toward the creation of such a court throughout the 1920s, and in 1926 the

---

intervention and trial. In October 1989, it was alleged that the US and the Soviet Union entered into a secret stipulation to contain terrorism. The stipulation, it was further alleged, provided that differences between the two nations concerning terrorism would be submitted to the ICJ for determination. This type of secret international politics sends a splintered message to all other nations and no message to the supporters and creators of terrorism.

81. Benjamin Ferencz, *An International Criminal Court: A Step Toward World Peace* (Dobbs Ferry, NY: Oceana Publications, 1980), p. 36.

International Law Association proposed both an international criminal court and a statute for the court to exercise separate jurisdiction in cases of states and individuals charged with international offenses. The law the proposed court would have applied would have consisted of international treaties and customs and judicial decisions where criminal behavior was recognized either in the proposed statutes of the court, the law of the residence of the defendant at the time of the commission of the crime or, failing that, the law of the state where the crime was committed.[82]

The economic collapse of the world in 1929 brought the efforts to create an international criminal court to a temporary close. In 1934, King Alexander of Yugoslavia was assassinated, and his assassin fled to Italy; the Italian government, in turn, refused to surrender the defendant for trial. The League of Nations responded in December 1934 by appointing a terrorism committee to study the issues created by the failure to extradite. As countries attempted to write a draft resolution, some viewed an international criminal court to cope with this type of problem as unnecessary; others deemed its proposed location too remote and inaccessible, and still others thought the court might be utilized to restrict freedom of expression or that it would be applied to armed conflict. And so the concept died once again. In 1950, the Report of the International Law Commission of the United Nations, in formulating the Nuremberg Principles, once again proposed an international criminal court.[83] What evolved was the European Court of Human Rights, which served as a model for the development of the Inter-American Court of Human Rights in 1979, but it was not a criminal court.

In December 1970, 50 nations became signatories to a Convention in the Hague for the Suppression of Unlawful Seizure of Aircraft. That same year, there was renewed interest in the creation of an international criminal court, but although there was an increase in hijacking and the deliberate massacre of thousands of people in Bangladesh, most nations turned away from the creation of this court and looked instead to the

---

82. International Law Association Report (London: Sweet & Maxwell, Ltd., 1927).
83. United Nations, General Assembly, Fifth Session Supplement, no.12 (A/1316) 1950.

safety and procedures of their own court systems. In 1982, at the 60th conference of the International Law Association, a draft statute for an international criminal court was once again presented and discussed.[84] It has not been adopted.

Again, my suggestion is not the creation of an additional international court, but the use of the established court and its present overall structure, with modifications and procedures to be applied to a narrowly focused issue—international extradition and terrorism. In addition, the International Court of Justice is presently operating in a world much different than it was as recently as two years ago, a world in which the East and West are not merely talking of accommodation but are making clear and hard movement towards it and the creation of obvious mechanisms for confidence-building measures. What was not accepted in the past is not suggested for the present. What is needed is a pragmatic series of small steps, implemented one at a time, that will have a greater chance of ultimately achieving, both politically and legally, the underlying aims of an international criminal court. In the spring of 1990, US and Soviet negotiators recognized that it would be difficult to conclude an agreement among *many* nations accepting binding judgment by the ICJ. They proposed that they first agree to specific terms and, when an agreement between them was completed, to ask the three remaining permanent members of the United Nations Security Council to adhere to its terms. The five nations would then appeal to other countries to join them. The immediate problem that has put the entire proposal in jeopardy is the attempt to place not only seven treaties dealing with terrorism and narcotics into the package to be agreed upon, but also to include other peripheral issues along with "opting-out" provisions that are "so broad that they could be invoked to exclude almost any case."[85]

What is suggested in this paper as a first step is that the major world players (to be followed by the balance of the membership of the United Nations) initially commit themselves to openly accept ICJ jurisdiction in matters involving

---

84. Report of the 60th Conference of the International Law Association (1983).
85. "World Court Plan Meets Difficulties," *The New York Times*, June 24, 1990, p. 9.

terrorism only, with the adoption of simplified court procedures that will address the sensitive issue of international extradition by outlining the following unambiguous procedures, to be followed without exception:

1. The executive branch of each government will determine whether a requesting nation seeking extradition has created false evidence in order to seek custody of a defendant it claims has committed a terrorist attack.

2. There will exist a rebuttable presumption that any victim of an attack is a civilian if he or she is not visibly identified by uniform, badge, or other visual marker or is not carrying a gun, concealed or otherwise. Excluded from this class of civilians are those persons, although not in uniform or with other visible marker, who have been publicly acknowledged as employees of government holding a rank or position that entails the exercise of individual judgment or discretion.

3. A nation seeking extradition will have the initial burden of proof, employing a standard higher than the common civil standard of evidence, that the victim of an attack was a civilian. If the crime alleged by the requesting nation is neither political on its face nor is the event clearly of a political character, then the requesting nation shall have no further burden of proof, except as provided in paragraph 4.[86]

4. In the event the incident claimed as support for extradition falls under paragraphs two and three and:

   a. the defendant is a citizen of the requesting state at the time of the alleged criminal act, then the requested hearing magistrate shall submit the entire matter to the ICJ for a final determination on the question of political exception and extradition. If the victim is a noncivilian, the entire matter is transferred to the ICJ to determine not only the political exception defense but also other extenuating circumstances, such as the harshness of the punishment in the requesting nation for the crime alleged;[87]

   b. the defendant is a citizen of the requested state or a naturalized citizen of that state at the time the alleged criminal act occurred, then the hearing magistrate shall conduct a hearing (utilizing a criminal standard of proof) on both the issue concerning identity of the person injured

---

86. The issue of burden of proof in regard to extradition is discussed in *Abu Eain v. Adams*, 529 F. Supp. 687 (N.D. Ill. 1980).
87. Note that this is one of the very few defenses the UK will entertain in an application for extradition.

or killed and the property attacked (civilian or not), and the political exception defense. An indispensable party to the proceeding would be the requesting state. If it is proven beyond a reasonable doubt (using the criminal standard of proof) that the victims were civilian, the entire matter would be transferred to the ICJ for further extradition proceedings. If the victim injured or killed is proved not to be a civilian, as defined above, the political exception issue would be determined initially by the hearing magistrate. Either side would have the right to take an adverse determination to the ICJ;

    c. the defendant is not a citizen of either the requesting or requested country, he or she shall be extradited to the country of his or her citizenship, pending an extradition hearing before ICJ.

It is the intention of this proposal that, in all instances except one, the extradition hearing and political exception issues will have a neutral base created through international cooperation and determined in the ICJ. International civilized conduct is to be supported by all nations, competing or not. This will be accomplished by not permitting the use of a nationally biased political exception rule or policy to prevent extradition when the object of the defendant's violence is a civilian population. Nations must recognize that acts that were "punishable even in the context of a declared war or in the heat of open military conflict" can never be condoned on political grounds.[88] If the atrocities of My Lai or Bataan cannot be tolerated by the legal institutions of a country, then, clearly, nor can those terrorist acts aimed at random civilian targets.

■ *Extradition Through International Control and Mutual Support*

The next step necessary for the containment of terrorism must be a coerced form of extradition. The *Achille Lauro* incident is a pure example of two countries, under intense internal and external pressure, walking a politically untenable tightrope. On the one hand, Egypt and Italy were bound to another nation by the terms of an extradition treaty.

---

88. *In re Doherty*, 599 F.Supp. 270 (S.D.N.Y. 1984), 615 F.Supp.755 (S.D.N.Y. 1985).

On the other hand, each feared terrorism. The proposal discussed above weaves together a modified political exception rule and a system of mutual international support when extradition is demanded. Through international cooperation, all parties would turn to the ICJ after a preliminary investigation and accept, without reservation, the same rules of extradition and definition of political exception.

If one were to follow the *Lauro* incident to its logical conclusion, each nation would have the right to unilaterally determine, as Italy did, the quantum of proof necessary for extradition on an ad hoc basis. That process becomes exposed to international pressures from other interested parties, and extradition becomes not only a meaningless tool but a sham. What is required, therefore, is a common set of criteria that will determine the grounds and quantum of proof necessary to support a request for extradition. If all nations are bound to a single system of extradition, mutual expectations would be supported through a single neutral international forum, the ICJ.

What is required for extradition is a judicial forum with international jurisdiction and recognition and with the ability to move quickly and decisively, utilizing uniform and accepted standards. To create yet another international court (an international criminal court), as noted above, would create, in addition to other problems, unnecessary and additional confusion in its formation, organization, and procedure. The approach proposed here is not only more economical but more intellectually efficient. Three judges of the ICJ would constitute a panel "on demand" to hear on an expedited basis all applications for extradition, such as that requested by the United States in *Lauro*. One of the three judges would be appointed on a rotating basis; the other two would be chosen, one each, by the requesting and requested state. Upon application for an extradition hearing before the ICJ, on notice to the parties, the defendant would automatically be frozen in position: he or she could not leave the requested state, and all other states would deny him or her entry until determination by the ICJ on the application of extradition.

This method not only gives notice that all states will adhere to a common substantive and procedural method in extradition proceedings of persons claimed to be terrorists, but also reduces the opportunity or chance for third parties to pressure the haven-nation to bend its laws to fit their threat. All nations, East and West, become part of the total process by closing their borders to terrorists, forming a protective cloak around the nation that might otherwise be intimidated. In addition, this method of international cooperation, along with other cooperative measures both in security and economics, will help lessen the tensions created by international terrorism.

3

Domestic Surveillance

■ *The Need For Domestic Surveillance*

Increased international cooperation between East and West has been based not merely upon the goodwill of the parties, but also on the wide variety of intelligence information available to each side about the other. Intelligence officers of all governments are required not only to understand the present intentions of their allies, enemies and potential enemies, but also their unspoken and hidden future agendas. In addition, intelligence officers are required to anticipate the future intelligence requirements and needs of their own countries, determining the meaning of the information collected, the meaning of the information that *will be* needed, the parties who may have that information, and whether it exists at all. "For the intelligence community there is simply more politics in the world to cover than ever before."[89]

In the political world of 1990 it would appear to be inconceivable that terrorist attacks against the West would find their genesis in the East. The continuing revelations in 1990 of state-generated abuses in Eastern Europe have so shocked the people of those nations as to foreclose the use of terrorism by their emerging governments. In other parts of the world, however, not only are there "today relatively small groups (that) can generate enough violence . . . (to) create incendiary

---

89. Bruce D. Berkowitz and Allan E. Goodman, *Strategic Intelligence* (Princeton: Princeton University Press, 1989), p. 15. This work discusses the complexity of turning raw data into useful information.

situations,"[90] but the eruption of the Iraqi invasion of Kuwait and the US presence in Saudi Arabia have produced an apparently sympathetic and voluntary terrorist force for Saddam Hussein to evidence their solidarity with the Iraqi leader or possibly to curry his favor. It has been reported that Abu Iyad (an Arafat deputy) has moved to Iraq, bringing with him members of Arafat's elite Force 17.[91]

While it is true that intelligence collection problems can be and will be more and more sophisticated with advanced technology,[92] one problem will remain totally unchanged. Electronic surveillance, with all its moral and legal implications, is, by its very definition, an uninvited and unknown intrusion into a person's private world.[93] On the other hand, there are primary purposes for all types of intelligence surveillance that must be engaged in by any rational society:

1. Gaining information necessary to the defense of a state;
2. Gaining information necessary to the foreign affairs of state;
3. Enforcing a state's domestic criminal laws; and
4. Providing other states with information learned during the course of gathering intelligence pursuant to the first three purposes, which, for the sake of international cooperation and humanitarian considerations, should be conveyed to a state that is targeted for a criminal act such as an act of terrorism.

All governments must balance all these very real demands in order to protect their own territory and population (namely *all persons* found within their borders), and, at the same moment, insure the utmost freedom of all forms of expression and travel.

While at first blush the linkage between counter-espionage and counter-terrorism may appear to be close, with overlapping concerns by law enforcement authorities, the patterns of behavior of the potential defendant-spy are dissimilar to that of the terrorist. Although a review of the counter-espionage literature may be enlightening, it is submitted that counter-terrorism produces sufficiently distinct intelligence problems

---

90. Steven Metz, "An American Strategy for Low-Intensity Conflict," p. 11.
91. "In Baghdad: A Welcome Mat For Terrorists," *Newsweek*, September 3, 1990, p. 41.
92. Berkowitz and Goodman, *Strategic Intelligence*.
93. See generally Crenshaw, *Terrorism, Legitimacy and Power*.

and mandates a separate focus and analysis.[94] Realistically, there will be continuing challenges to the intelligence demands created by domestically- and internationally-inspired and supported terrorism.[95] It is universally recognized that public disclosure or recognition of the potential risk of surveillance of a person or group as a security risk will discourage many persons within and beyond the scope of the group from expressing their views on sensitive issues and will chill their rights.

This cannot mean that all electronic surveillance should or must be abandoned. Recognizing that electronic surveillance is never fully compatible with civil rights, the Canadian government, in its efforts to balance its intelligence demands and its obligation to protect the integrity of its citizens' civil rights, has developed a method of domestic surveillance that recognizes the dangers of unbridled intelligence exploring.[96] The Canadians accept the status of a standing quasi-judicial body to investigate, on an ongoing basis, complaints of excessive security surveillance. That body not only reviews the performance of the Security Service, but interacts with the entire Canadian intelligence network and reports to the parliament and the public all the information that national security would allow them to reveal.

Electronic surveillance need not lead automatically to civil rights abuses or tarnish a nation's integrity as a democracy.[97] In addition, it can produce international cooperation to contain international terrorism. What must first be overcome is the legacy of electronic surveillance worldwide, which has a long and grey history that has produced extremes in success and abuse. It has been unabashedly overused and employed by governments—playing "Big Brother"—to suppress valid, honest and objective thought, political movements and positions of

---

94. See Crelinsten, "Terrorism, Counter-Terrorism and Democracy."
95. Recent examples include the 1989 capture of Kikumura with five bombs in New Jersey, Hussein's threat in July 1990 to use poison gas against Israeli and US interests, and terrorists volunteering their service to Hussein in September of 1990.
96. Canadian Security Intelligence Service Act (CSIS).
97. Electronic surveillance is the acquisition by an electronic, mechanical or other surveillance device of the contents of any wire or radio communication or to acquire information other than from a wire or radio communication under circumstances in which a person has reasonable expectations of privacy.

dissent. It has been utilized to blackmail and silence persons of the highest integrity, to prevent or suppress dissent, or to protect vested interests. Notwithstanding the very real fears and the long, lingering echoes of serious and, at times, outrageous surveillance abuses by various governments, including the US, this history should not be seized upon to completely smother an otherwise appropriate and effective preventive, defensive tool.

The proposals made in this chapter do not argue that, where there is a potential for a serious terrorist crisis, a surveillance plan should ignore or circumvent broadly protected individual rights. In addition, the discussion that evolves from these proposals should not focus on the issue of morality as a bright line in determining the use of electronic surveillance. For example, what should not be considered in evaluating the proposal is the morality or legitimate goals of the target of surveillance. It is immaterial whether you are "for or against" the Catholic or Protestant position in Northern Ireland or whether you live in Boston rather than Philadelphia. "Terrorism can be judged on two levels: the morality of the ends and the morality of the means."[98] Ultimately, it is the means the actor employs—the threat or use of acts of serious violence against civilians or civilian property or installations—that should determine the propriety of electronic surveillance, with no regard to the morality, or even legitimacy, of the ends sought. With the increasing number of targets present and potential—from the traditional forums of violence to the drug lords—it is intelligence data that forms the basic instrument employed by a state to plan its international and domestic posture and defense. However one may define intelligence gathering or view the intelligence cycle,[99] it comes down to, despite Henry Stimson's reservations, gentlemen reading other gentlemen's mail.

---

98. Crenshaw, *Terrorism, Legitimacy, and Power*.
99. The intelligence cycle refers to the method or steps through which raw information is "converted into intelligence" and thus made available and useful to the user. It includes operational intelligence (required for planning and executing all types of operations), critical intelligence (information that has been analyzed and that is required immediately in order for timely responses to be available; it is synonymous with tactical intelligence), and strategic intelligence (information required to formulate or develop long-range plans of a wide scope, as opposed to tactical intelligence, which is narrow in scope and shorter in focus).

■ The Sleeper and International Cooperation

While any policy toward the containment of espionage, guerrilla warfare, or terrorism has its costs to a country and its inhabitants, a narrow but important issue is the containment of a species of terrorism practiced by a sleeper. The very nature of the activities of a sleeper, prior to the actual execution of his or her criminal act of terrorism, presents special considerations and problems not addressed in the Foreign Intelligence Surveillance Act of 1978.[100] A sleeper is a person who is *not* a US citizen by birth but an alien who is lawfully in the US (i.e., he or she has not entered the US illegally and presumably has a valid foreign passport issued by a foreign government).[101] The sleeper is present in the US with or without permanent status and may at the time of the commission of his criminal act be a naturalized US citizen. A sleeper's initial task, operation or mission, upon entry into the US, is to become assimilated into the fabric of society and its work force. There will be no hard evidence that a sleeper has been trained in foreign espionage that would require him or her to register with the US government.[102] Nor is a sleeper a person who is normally thought of as being subject to the act that controls subversive activities.[103] A sleeper is not a mole (a person employed by one government, not knowing that the "mole" is employed by another government for the purposes of spying or to plant misinformation). Nor is the sleeper in the US as a saboteur (to blow up a military installation or nuclear plant).[104] The sleeper is not in the US to kill a member of Congress or the Cabinet or a Justice of the Supreme Court of the United States. Nor is it the intent of a sleeper to take hostages.

The role of the sleeper *is to wait.* To wait while he or she is accepted by and becomes part of the local community; to await

---

100. 50 USCA §1801 et seq.
101. Obviously, if the target is unlawfully in the US, the full force of a criminal investigation is at the disposal of the authorities.
102. 50 USCA § 851. Failure to register would constitute a federal crime and, consequently, would support an application for an order granting electronic surveillance.
103. 50 USCA § 781. The following activities are subject to this act: conspiracy or attempt to establish a totalitarian dictatorship or the communication of classifed information or the receipt of classified information by a foreign agent.
104. 18 USCA § 2151 et seq. See also Appendix A.

the receipt of orders from his or her handler, which may take months and even years to arrive. In the interim, a sleeper may train or prepare to commit or facilitate a violent criminal act defined as terrorism, to strike at nonmilitary, nongovernmental installations or civilians in the name of his or her sponsor or cause. It is obvious from this short description that a sleeper may go through extremely long periods of time when there is no present or active criminal conspiracy or present engagement in a criminal act that could legally support an order or warrant for electronic surveillance.[105] In other words, for extended periods of time there may not be a clearly recognized smoking gun. Nor may there be the type of conduct or evidence that could trigger the use of the Foreign Intelligence Surveillance Act of 1978 as a method to support an order of surveillance. In the UK, Paul Wilkinson, Chairperson of the Research Foundation for the Study of Terrorism, complained publicly of the "yawning intelligence gap" that permits the IRA to export terrorism to Britain with its employment of sleepers to spread their violence.[106]

The sleeper in the United States is no less an international terrorist than if he or she attacked a US interest abroad rather than in New York. The danger of a sleeper in action is that there will be no action for long periods of time, or the conduct engaged in may be so obscure (because it is extended over long period of time) that unless the actions are reviewed by surveillance over similar time periods, information recovered at any one moment may not, upon analysis, indicate the preparation for an event or goal constituting terrorism. A purely international terrorist act is not an immediate, spontaneous-combustion event; to the contrary, it is neither spontaneous nor quickly organized. Its modus operandi is to have the fewest number of persons (of the entire membership) engaged in the planning and execution of the attack. The ultimate working conditions for a terrorist group are to have the planning and execution phases of the attack organized and executed by separate small groups, none knowing the identity of the members of the other "cells". While a sleeper is a terrorist, not all terrorists are

---

105. A wiretap application (18 USCA §2518) must show "probable cause" that the target has or is about to commit one of several crimes. *Probable cause* indicates that there is more objective reason to believe than not that an event has taken place or will take place.
106. *Newsweek*, August 13, 1990, pp. 42–43.

sleepers. As opposed to a person with discernible ties to a terrorist group (who is not integrated into mainstream society), the sleeper, of all the terrorists, is the most integrated and therefore least obvious, least noticeable "member" of a terrorist group, and consequently, potentially the most dangerous.[107] There is seemingly nothing in the daily activity of the sleeper that would attract the attention of the intelligence community, and thus he or she is overlooked. Therefore, a different statutory, legally supportable method of obtaining intelligence is required to contain, minimize or reduce the chances of a successful sleeper attack. As the saying goes, you do not have your initial fire drill during a fire.

Michael Ledeen, the author of *Perilous Statecraft* who, at the direction of the White House, was personally involved in the negotiations with the Italian government during the *Lauro* hijacking, has noted that there have been large numbers of sleeper groups placed in the US by foreign entities.[108]

Another expert, Steven Emerson, has also noted that the East German Stasi, long recognized "as one of the most effective intelligence services in the world," had strong ties to terrorist groups, including the PLO, France's Action Directe, and the Basque separatist group ETA. The Libyan connection, he notes, was "especially close" to the Stasi. Referring to spies and terrorists, he reports that there are at least 500 persons dispatched by the Stasi whose identities are unknown and who may "sign up with new masters." They "will adopt a low profile, patiently waiting, as they have been indoctrinated to do, for the time when they can once again ply their trade." He quotes a West German government official as describing the situation as a "nightmare".[109]

With electronic surveillance as proposed, not only is it possible to prevent and thus contain an act of violence, but the material learned by reason of the intelligence may also provide the vital connection between the defendant and sponsor. In addition, if the sponsor is a government, or is supported or controlled by a government, then a country such as the US would have several options. The most important is direct

---

107. *Newsweek*, August 13, 1990, pp. 42–43, discusses the IRA's use of sleepers in Britain.
108. Michael Ledeen, interview with the author, September 10, 1990.
109. Steven Emerson, "Where Have All the Spies Gone?" *The New York Times Magazine*, August 12, 1990, p. 16.

communication with the offending nation. Sufficient evidence would be revealed—without the full disclosure that may reveal its surveillance "tradecraft"—to show the attempted act and the connection to the offending nation, coupled with a demand for compliance with international law. The alternative is wide public denunciation of the claimed violation. This approach accomplishes several goals:

1. It places the sponsoring nation in a defensive position, with the hope that it will move away from this form of activity.
2. If the violent act contemplated by the sleeper has been intercepted prior to execution, then the discussions between countries take place in an atmosphere of less tension.
3. The country that was to be the target can initially enter into discussions with the sponsor in an atmosphere free of public pressure exerted by its own citizens.
4. If the sponsor indicates a refusal to refrain from the use of terrorism as a means of diplomacy, then the last resort will be the public disclosure of the violation and the warning of future action that may include force.

■ *Statutory Proposal on the Sleeper As the Target*

A. Introduction

If a sleeper is successful, law enforcement has failed, since it did not identify and capture beforehand those involved. The act has occurred. For this reason, electronic surveillance is obviously necessary. The method adopted, however, must generate the least amount of invasion into the privacy of not only the individuals in communication with the sleeper, but also the sleeper himself. Therefore, in choosing a sleeper as the possible target for electronic surveillance, the decision must be viewed in both legal and prudent terms. The first consideration: What are the target's legal rights? The second: Is it strictly necessary to investigate electronically a particular person who obviously neither lives nor works in a vacuum?

A targeting procedure must contain both independent oversight and supervision procedures. Although the target will be ignorant of the petition seeking an order for electronic surveillance, there will be, under the proposal made in this chapter, the automatic appointment of an independent legal counsel whose task it is to protect and defend against the initial granting or continuance of an electronic surveillance warrant or order. As discussed below, with the creation of an oversight agency and an independent advocate's office, there will be ongoing protection of the legal rights of both the target and those persons in communication with the target. This method should reduce the veil of suspicion and acrimony that appears from time to time between Congress and the intelligence community—a confrontation that leads eventually to a shortened leash on the latter group, with demoralizing long-term results to intelligence gathering. Finally, the proposed method will also reduce the blunders and misconceptions inherent in any surveillance operation. The proposed system will demonstrably protect the civil rights of all persons within a real and practical framework.

B. Proposed Surveillance Statute

As presently constituted, the Foreign Intelligence Surveillance Act, as interpreted by the federal courts,[110] limits its mandate to the initial collection of intelligence for national security purposes, and is not an initial tool for the collection of evidence needed for a criminal prosecution. This paper's proposal is to amend the Foreign Intelligence Surveillance Act of 1978 to permit *long-term, judicially ordered* electronic surveillance within the US of certain narrowly defined persons under the following conditions:

1. The persons to be placed under surveillance must fit one of several sleeper profiles.[111] These profiles, which will be reviewed and passed upon by the appropriate congressional committees, will be developed by intelligence officers and will be based on behavior manifested in past terrorist cases.
2. There must be independent evidence that would support the

---

110. *U.S. v. Megahey,* 553 F. Supp. 1180, affd. 729 F.3d 1444 (D.C.N.Y. 1982), *Matter of Kevork,* 634 F. Supp. 1015 (C.D.Ca. 1985).
111. A profile is a set of activities or facts that have previously been agreed upon and tested, which if exhibited by a person would lead to the reasonable conclusion with a high degree of probability that this person was engaged in or was about to engage in a particular activity/conduct. It will be necessary to review the profiles developed as conditions change and as new actors are introduced.

"assumption"—not the conclusion or even a finding of probable cause—that the target was *trained* in or was conducting himself or herself in a manner that would indicate an intent to commit a terrorist act in the US. The evidence standard would be less than is required to support the usual evidentiary test for granting such an order as noted above, but what would be required would be something more than mere conjecture or hunch.

i. Institutions[112]

Two new institutions would be created and developed to protect the rights of the target and those in communication with the target:

1. The US Senate and House of Representatives, through a Joint Oversight Committee (JOC), would establish an Oversight Agency, which would consist of an oversight director and staff. This agency would serve at the discretion of the JOC. The powers and duties of the Oversight Agency and its legal staff would be to review the work of the Target Advocate's Office (below). The agency would review all surveillance material collected by any federal law enforcement or intelligence agency pursuant to an electronic surveillance order under the proposed amendment. As described below, the agency would determine what surveillance material would be retained, and would supervise the destruction of gathered surveillance material that is found to have no relevance with regard to a particular target or those in communication with the target. It would prepare reports to the JOC on a yearly basis or as demanded. Lastly, it would review complaints from targets.

2. Congress would also establish the Target Advocate's Office, consisting of a director who should be appointed for a fixed term of five years by the president, with the consent of Congress. The powers and duties of the Advocate's Office and its staff of regional attorneys would be to provide automatic legal representation to a target prior to and during all steps leading to the granting of an order of electronic surveillance, its continuance, its termination and the destruction of surveillance records or the indictment of the target.

---

112. None of the recommendations contained in this part envisions the creation of a large bureaucratic web, and none would be needed or desirable.

ii. Basis for Long-Term Order

The basis for an electronic surveillance order, pursuant to the proposal in this paper, cannot be premised solely upon lawful advocacy, protest or dissent *unless* the surveillance is carried out to investigate an activity that, objectively, could be reasonably calculated to lead to or to constitute a violent act contrary to the criminal laws of the US. For example, to advocate the position that the present US policy in the Middle East is reprehensible and must be immediately altered or changed, cannot as a matter of law support a surveillance order under this act. Nor would a surveillance order be placed against a person who advocates that, with the change in demographics in the US, foreign-born non-US citizens in the US represent the true defenders of national integrity because of their labor and low economic status and thus deserve the right to vote. The same conduct, but with a call for funds to purchase weapons or with the purchase of material that could be utilized in a violent offensive capability, would be sufficient to support an order of surveillance. To employ the Kikumura case as an example: If his identity and the material he had purchased had been uncovered halfway through his circuitous shopping route for explosive material, and if, in addition, he fit the necessary profile, a long-term electronic surveillance would have been permitted under this proposal.

iii. Procedure

The process begins with an application and certification by the US Attorney General establishing the basis and need for an extended electronic surveillance order directed at a particular target. The Attorney General's application, without notification to the intended target, would be filed with a judge of the Federal Circuit Court for the circuit within which the target is domiciled. A copy of the certification, application and all other papers submitted to the court would then be served upon both the Oversight Agency and the Advocate's Office. No judge would entertain the government's application of extended electronic surveillance or its continuance without the presence of an attorney from the Advocate's Office. The Attorney General's documentation in support of the application would include the certification to the court that investigation procedures other than electronic surveillance have been utilized and have failed or were unlikely to succeed in determining the target's ultimate intentions, and that extended electronic surveillance was likely to be the only additional method to determine the legality of the target's activities within the US. Lastly, the Attorney General must have *supportable* information that would reasonably lead to the conclusion that the target is a sleeper. In addition, the government must show that the urgency of the matter is such that it would be impractical to continue with other investigative procedures without the added support mechanism of electronic surveillance. The Attorney General must provide *supportable* reasons for the extended time period of the surveillance requested.

At the termination of the hearing for the initial surveillance order or its continuance, the court's determination and the papers upon which it was made would be forwarded to the Oversight Agency.

If an order of surveillance is granted, the Oversight Agency would conduct a periodic review of all the surveillance records of a particular target. In consultation with the Attorney General's Office, electronic records would be destroyed, including any written records made from information learned from the electronic records. This would include the identity of persons who have been recorded communicating with the target and any other information that has no legitimate purpose in the investigation of the target, or of terrorism or other criminal activity.[113] If there is disagreement with regard to the destruction of information and records, the court that granted the surveillance warrant or order would, upon notification to all parties (Attorney General's Office, Target Advocate's Office and Oversight Agency), determine the propriety of further maintenance of the contested information.[114] The party desiring to retain the records would have the initial burden of demonstrating the necessity for its safekeeping.

For other than a criminal prosecution or future investigation, there will be a prohibition against disclosure of any

---

113. What is thought of in this category are those cases in which terrorism and the drug trade are linked. It was reported that a cocaine dealer in Colombia ordered three car bombings in civilian areas that killed 26 people and wounded 178. *The New York Times,* May 14, 1990, p. A3.
114. There is at present no federal agency that has the authority to order another federal agency to alter or change its activities or destroy documentation.

information contained in the electronic surveillance records or learned by reason of the surveillance records, or the identity of any person who is either identified in the electronic records as the target or who communicates with the target. Any such disclosures would constitute a criminal act.

iv. Surveillance Targets

This act would *not*, under any circumstances, be available to direct electronic surveillance against any person who is a US citizen by birth or who has been a naturalized citizen for a period of five or more years, or permanent aliens who shall have been domiciled in the United States for ten or more years at the time of the application for an order of electronic surveillance. All other persons will be subject to electronic surveillance either because of their profile or because of evidence as described above.

Although it may appear that the proposal is unwieldy because of the number of persons who will have direct (and unannounced) involvement in the surveillance of each target, it is submitted that without a method to protect the target's legal interests, a necessary, meaningful and valid tool of intelligence will be constitutionally unacceptable.

CONCLUSION

Terrorism cannot be eradicated; it can merely be contained. At present, the degree of containment is in large part dependent at any given moment upon international goodwill and success in weaving together the political aims of the parties involved. To construct a workable system of containment of international terrorism, there must be, as a first step, a program that views terrorism as impermissible violence, whatever the motives, when directed against any civilian target. There must also be a program that reduces the power of individual nations in determining those grounds and defenses that may be interposed against international terrorism extradition. Most importantly, each nation must execute a firm, irrevocable commitment to a neutral decision making body that will determine all the conditions for international extradition of terrorists. In addition, to reduce the tensions created by terrorism, methods of electronic surveillance (with appropriate safeguards) must be available to each government.

The fear of violence produced in a city by drugs, economic fear or violent racial tension produces an emotional paralysis and local paranoia that drive people to quit their neighborhoods, remain locked in their homes, or create civilian vigilante groups. The dynamics and structure of a city in fear of violence is but a microcosm of the destructive effect created internationally by nondomestic terrorism. Through meaningful cooperation beyond public rhetoric,[115] nations must enter into binding agreements to move toward greater containment of terrorism.

---

115. Europe, with a single market of 336 million people by the end of 1992, will remain a group of separate sovereign nation-states if they continue to conduct their foreign affairs as they did during the Persian Gulf crisis by failing to act as one economic force to bring pressure to bear in that region.

Appendix A
Selected Definitions

ESPIONAGE. The use of spies to discover the secrets of another nation. A mole is one species of spy, but one who is *employed* by one government that does know that the person (mole) is actually engaged by another government for the purposes of spying or planting misinformation.

FREE FIRE-ZONE. A geographic area within which weapon fire is expected, and all persons entering the area are presumed to have assumed the risk of injury or death.

GUERRILLA WARFARE. Warfare used by an irregular army employing the technique of surprise attack and harassment to weaken a regular army.

POLITICAL EXCEPTION RULE. Rule invoked by a defendant who seeks to defeat an international extradition proceeding by claiming that his or her "crime" was politically motivated and thus exempt from criminal prosecution and extradition.

PROBABLE CAUSE. Objective reason to believe, based upon the evidence presented to a court, that a criminal event has taken place or is about to take place.

PROFILE. A set of activities or facts, previously agreed upon and tested, which, if exhibited by a person, would lead to the reasonable conclusion that the person who "fit" the profile was engaged in or was about to engage in a particular activity.

SABOTAGE. In the US (18 USCA § 2151 et seq.), the deliberate destruction of certain types of statutorily defined and identified property, e.g., military installations, specific industrial sites, communications facilities, transportation facilities. The term derives from the French word "sabot" (wooden shoe) that French workers threw into new machinery in the early stages of the Industrial Revolution in the hopes of preventing unemployment.

SLEEPER. A person who is lawfully in the US, but not a citizen, who seeks to become assimilated into the fabric of society and waits for directions to commit an act of violence against individual civilians or against civilian property or installations.

TERRORISM.
1. A particular strategy of political communication. It utilizes a combination of violence and the threat of violence. Ronald Crelinstsen, "Terrorism, Counter-Terrorism and Threat of Violence," *Terrorism and Political Violence* 1, no.2, April 1989.
2. Indiscriminate acts of violence whose aim is to have a psychological effect out of proportion to its purely physical result. Raymond Aron, *Peace and War* (New York: Weidenfeld & Nicolson, 1966), p.170.
3. Highly visible violence directed against randomly selected civilians in an effort to generate a pervasive sense of fear and thus affect government

policies. Jay Shafritz et al, *The Facts on File Dictionary of Military Science* (New York: Facts on File, 1989).

4. Premeditated, politically motivated violence perpetrated against noncombatant targets by subnational groups or clandestine state agents, usually intended to influence an audience. International terrorism is terrorism involving the citizens or territory of more than one country. US Department of State, 1989. (These are two of a total of close to 60 definitions made by the US government).

5. See the US Foreign Intelligence Surveillance Act of 1987 (Appendix B).

Appendix B
Selected Sections of Statutes and Treaties

from the **Charter of the United Nations**

Article 2, Paragraph 4

All Members shall refrain in their international relations from the threat or use of force against the territorial integrity or political independence of any state, or in any other manner inconsistent with the Purposes of the United Nations.

from the **Declaration on Principles of International Law Concerning Friendly Relations and Cooperation Among States in Accordance With the Charter of the United Nations (Resolution 2625 (XXV))**

Every State has the duty to refrain from organizing or encouraging the organization of irregular forces or armed bands, including mercenaries, for incursion into the territory of another State.

Every State has the duty to refrain from organizing, instigating, assisting or participating in acts of civil strife or terrorist acts in another State or acquiescing in organized activities within its territory directed towards the commission of such acts, when the acts referred to in the present paragraph involve a threat or use of force.

from the **UN Security Council resolution of August 25, 1990, authorizing military action to halt all maritime trade with Iraq:**

The Security Council . . . [c]alls upon those member states cooperating with the Government of Kuwait which are deploying maritime forces to the area to use such measures commensurate to the specific circumstances as may be necessary under the authority of the Security Council to halt all inward and outward maritime shipping in order to inspect and verify their cargoes and destinations and to insure strict implementation of the provisions related to such shipping laid down in Resolution 661 (1990).

from the **Foreign Intelligence Surveillance Act**

1801. Definitions
c. "International terrorism" means activities that—
    1. involve violent acts or acts dangerous to human life that are a violation of the criminal laws of the United States or of any State, or that would be a criminal violation if committed within the jurisdiction of the United States or any State;

2. appear to be intended—
  A. to intimidate or coerce a civilian population;
  B. to influence the policy of a government by intimidation or coercion; or
  C. to affect the conduct of a government by assassination or kidnapping; and
3. occur totally outside the United States or transcend national boundaries in terms of the means by which they are accomplished, the persons they appear intended to coerce or intimidate, or the locale in which their perpetrators operate or seek asylum. . . .
e. "Foreign intelligence information" means—
  1. information that relates to, and if concerning a United States person is necessary to, the ability of the United States to protect against—
    A. actual or potential attack or other grave hostile acts of a foreign power or an agent of a foreign power;
    B. sabotage or international terrorism by a foreign power or an agent of a foreign power; or
    C. clandestine intelligence activities by an intelligence service or network of a foreign power or by an agent of a foreign power; or
  2. information with respect to a foreign power or foreign territory that relates to, and if concerning a United States person is necessary to—
    A. the national defense or the security of the United States; or
    B. the conduct of the foreign affairs of the United States.
f. "Electronic surveillance" means—
  1. the acquisition by an electronic, mechanical, or other surveillance device of the contents of any wire or radio communication sent by or intended to be received by a particular, known United States person who is in the United States, if the contents are acquired by intentionally targeting that United States person, under circumstances in which a person has a reasonable expectation of privacy and a warrant would be required for law enforcement purposes;
  2. the acquisition by an electronic, mechanical, or other surveillance device of the contents of any wire communication to or from a person in the United States, without the consent of any party thereto, if such acquisition occurs in the United States;
  3. the intentional acquisition by an electronic, mechanical, or other surveillance device of the contents of any radio communication, under circumstances in which a person has a reasonable expectation of privacy and a warrant would be required for law enforcement purposes, and if both the sender and all intended recipients are located within the United States; or
  4. the installation or use of an electronic, mechanical, or other surveillance device in the United States for monitoring to acquire information, other than from a wire or radio communication, under circumstances in which a person has a reasonable expectation of privacy and a warrant would be required for law enforcement purposes.

from the **Convention on Extradition Between the Government of the United States of America and the Government of the State of Israel**

Article I

Each Contracting Party agrees, under the conditions and circumstances established by the present Convention, reciprocally to deliver up persons found in its territory who have been charged with or convicted of any of the offenses mentioned in Article II of the present Convention committed within the territorial jurisdiction of the other, or outside thereof under the conditions specified in Article III of the present Convention.

Article II

Persons shall be delivered up according to the provisions of the present Convention for prosecution when they have been charged with, or to undergo sentence when they have been convicted of, any of the following offenses: 1) Murder; 2) Manslaughter; 3) Malicious wounding; inflicting grievous bodily harm; . . . 9) Kidnapping; abduction; false imprisonment; . . . 24) Arson; 25) Any malicious act done with intent to endanger the safety of any persons travelling upon a railway; 26) Piracy, by the law of nations; . . .

Extradition shall also be granted for attempts to commit or conspiracy to commit any of the offenses mentioned in this Article provided such attempts or such conspiracy are punishable under the laws of both Parties by a term of imprisonment exceeding three years.

Extradition shall also be granted for participation in any of the offenses mentioned in this Article.

Article III

When the offense has been committed outside the territorial jurisdiction of the requesting Party, extradition need not be granted unless the laws of the requested Party provide for the punishment of such an offense committed in similar circumstances. . . .

Article IV

A requested Party shall not decline to extradite a person sought because such person is a national of the requested Party.

Article V

Extradition shall be granted only if the evidence be found sufficient, according to the laws of the place where the person sought shall be found, either to justify his committal for trial if the offense of which he is accused had been committed in that place or to prove that he is the identical person convicted by the courts of the requesting Party.

Article VI

Extradition shall not be granted in any of the following circumstances:

1. When the person whose surrender is sought is being proceeded against, or has been tried and discharged or punished, in the territory of the requested Party for the offense for which his extradition is requested.
2. When the person whose surrender is sought has been tried and acquitted, or undergone his punishment, in a third State for the offense for which his extradition is requested.
3. When the prosecution or the enforcement of the penalty for the offense has become barred by lapse of time according to the laws of the requesting Party or would be barred by lapse of time according to the laws of the requested Party had the offense been committed in its territory.
4. When the offense is regarded by the requested Party as one of a political character or if the person sought proves that the request for his extradition has, in fact, been made with a view to trying or punishing him for an offense of a political character.

Article VII

When the offense for which the extradition is requested is punishable by death under the laws of the requesting Party and the laws of the requested Party do not permit such punishment for that offense, extradition may be refused unless the requesting Party provides such assurances as the requested Party considers sufficient that the death penalty shall not be imposed, or, if imposed, shall not be executed. . . .

Article XI

In case of urgency a Contracting Party may apply for the provisional arrest of the person sought pending the presentation of the request for extradition through the diplomatic channel. . . .

On receipt of such an application the requested Party shall take the necessary steps to secure the arrest of the person claimed.

A person arrested upon such an application shall be set at liberty upon the expiration of sixty days from the date of his arrest if a request for his extradition accompanied by the documents specified in Article X shall not have been received. However, this stipulation shall not prevent the institution of proceedings with a view to extraditing the person sought if the request is subsequently received.

from the Extradition Treaty Between the Government of the United States of America and the Government of the United Kingdom of Great Britain and Northern Ireland

Article I

Each Contracting Party undertakes to extradite to the other, in the circumstances and subject to the conditions specified in this Treaty, any person found in its territory who has been accused or convicted of any offense within Article III, committed within the jurisdiction of the other Party. . . .

Article III

1. Extradition shall be granted for an act or omission the facts of which disclose an offense within any of the descriptions listed in the Schedule annexed to this Treaty, which is an integral part of the Treaty, or any other offense, if:
   a. the offense is punishable under the laws of both Parties by imprisonment or other form of detention for more than one year or by the death penalty;
   b. the offense is extraditable under the relevant law, being the law of the United Kingdom or other territory to which this Treaty applies by virtue of sub-paragraph (1)(a) of Article II; and
   c. the offense constitutes a felony under the law of the United States of America.
2. Extradition shall also be granted for any attempt or conspiracy to commit an offense within paragraph (1) of this Article if such attempt or conspiracy is one for which extradition may be granted under the laws of both Parties and is punishable under the laws of both Parties by imprisonment or other form of detention for more than one year or by the death penalty.
3. Extradition shall also be granted for the offense of impeding the arrest or prosecution of a person who has committed an offense for which extradition may be granted under this Article and which is punishable under the laws of both Parties by imprisonment or other form of detention for a period of five years or more.
4. A person convicted of and sentenced for an offense shall not be extradited therefor unless he was sentenced to imprisonment or other form of detention for a period of four months or more or, subject to the provisions of Article IV, to the death penalty.

Article IV

If the offense for which extradition is requested is punishable by death under the relevant law of the requesting Party, but the relevant law of the requested party does not provide for the death penalty in a similar case, extradition may be refused unless the requesting Party gives assurances satisfactory to the requested Party that the death penalty will not be carried out.

Article V

1. Extradition shall not be granted if:
   a. the person sought would, if proceeded against in the territory of the requested Party for the offense for which his extradition is requested, be entitled to be discharged on the grounds of a previous acquittal or conviction in the territory of the requesting or requested Party or of a third State; or
   b. the prosecution for the offense for which extradition is requested has become barred by lapse of time according to the law of the requesting or requested Party; or
   c. (i)   the offense for which extradition is requested is regarded by the requested Party as one of a political character; or

(ii) the person sought proves that the request for his extradition has in fact been made with a view to try or punish him for an offense of a political character.

2. Extradition may be refused on any other ground which is specified by the law of the requested Party. . . .

Article VIII

1. In urgent cases the person sought may, in accordance with the law of the requested party, be provisionally arrested on application through the diplomatic channel by the competent authorities of the requesting Party. . . .

2. A person arrested upon such an application shall be set at liberty upon the expiration of forty-five days from the date of his arrest if a request for his extradition shall not have been received. This provision shall not prevent the institution of further proceedings for the extradition of the person sought if a request is subsequently received.

Article IX

1. Extradition shall be granted only if the evidence be found sufficient according to the law of the requested Party either to justify the committal for trial of the person sought if the offense of which he is accused had been committed in the territory of the requested Party or to prove that he is the identical person convicted by the courts of the requesting Party.

2. If the requested Party requires additional evidence or information to enable a decision to be taken on the request for extradition, such evidence or information shall be submitted within such time as that Party shall require.

Article X

If the extradition of a person is requested concurrently by one of the Contracting Parties and by another State or States, either for the same offense or for different offenses, the requested Party shall make its decision in so far as its law allows, having regard to all the circumstances, including the provisions in this regard in any Agreements in force between the requested Party and the requesting States, the relative seriousness and place of commission of the offenses, the respective dates of the requests, the nationality of the person sought and the possibility of subsequent extradition to another State.

Article XI

1. The requested Party shall promptly communicate to the requesting Party through the diplomatic channel the decision on the request for extradition.

2. If a warrant or order for the extradition of a person sought has been issued by the competent authority and he is not removed from the territory of the requested Party within such time as may be required under the law of that Party, he may be set at liberty and the requested Party may subsequently refuse to extradite him for the same offense.

Article XII

1. A person extradited shall not be detained or proceeded against in the territory of the requesting Party for any offense other than an extraditable offense established by the facts in respect of which his extradition has been granted, or on account of any other matters, nor be extradited by that Party to a third State—
   a. until after he has returned to the territory of the requested Party; or
   b. until the expiration of thirty days after he has been free to return to the territory of the requested Party.
2. The provisions of paragraph (1) of this Article shall not apply to offenses committed, or matters arising, after the extradition.

from the **Supplementary Treaty Concerning the Extradition Treaty Between the Government of the United States of America and the Government of the United Kingdom of Great Britain and Northern Ireland, Signed at London on 8 June 1972**

Article 1

For the purposes of the Extradition Treaty, none of the following offenses shall be regarded as an offense of a political character:
a. an offense within the scope of the Convention for the Suppression of Unlawful Seizure of Aircraft, opened for signature at The Hague on 16 December 1970;
b. an offense within the scope of the Convention for the Suppression of Unlawful Acts against the Safety of Civil Aviation, opened for signature at Montreal on 23 September 1971;
c. an offense within the scope of the Convention on the Prevention and Punishment of Crimes against Internationally Protected Persons, including Diplomatic Agents, opened for signature at New York on 14 December 1973;
d. an offense within the scope of the International Convention against the Taking of Hostages, opened for signature at New York on 18 December 1979;
e. murder;
f. manslaughter;
g. maliciously wounding or inflicting grievous bodily harm;
h. kidnapping, abduction, false imprisonment or unlawful detention, including the taking of a hostage;
i. the following offenses relating to explosives;
   1. the causing of an explosion likely to endanger life or cause serious damage to property; or
   2. conspiracy to cause such an explosion; or
   3. the making or possession of an explosive substance by a person who intends either himself or through another person to endanger life or cause serious damage to property;
j. the following offenses relating to firearms or ammunition:
   1. the possession of a firearm or ammunition by a person who intends either himself or through another person to endanger life; or

2. the use of a firearm by a person with intent to resist or prevent the arrest or detention of himself or another person;
k. damaging property with intent to endanger life or with reckless disregard as to whether the life of another would thereby be endangered;
l. an attempt to commit any of the foregoing offenses.

from the European Convention on Extradition

Article 1

Obligation to extradite

The Contracting Parties undertake to surrender to each other, subject to the provisions and conditions laid down in this Convention, all persons against whom the competent authorities of the requesting Party are proceeding for an offense or who are wanted by the said authorities for the carrying out of a sentence or detention order. . . .

Article 3

Political offenses

1. Extradition shall not be granted if the offense in respect of which it is required is regarded by the requested Party as a political offense or as an offense connected with a political offense.
2. The same rule shall apply if the requested Party has substantial grounds for believing that a request for extradition for an ordinary criminal offense has been made for the purpose of prosecuting or punishing a person on account of his race, religion, nationality or political opinion, or that that person's position may be prejudiced for any of these reasons.
3. The taking or attempted taking of the life of a Head of State or a member of his family shall not be deemed to be a political offense for the purposes of this Convention. . . .

Article 6

Extradition of nationals

1. a. A Contracting Party shall have the right to refuse extradition of its nationals. . . .

Article 7

Place of commission

1. The requested Party may refuse to extradite a person claimed for an offense which is regarded by its law as having been committed in whole or in part in its territory or in a place treated as its territory.

from the European Convention on the Suppression of Terrorism

Article 1

For the purposes of extradition between contracting states none of the following offenses shall be regarded as a political offense. . . :

a. an offense within the scope of the Convention for the Suppression of Unlawful Seizure of Aircraft, signed at The Hague on 16 December 1970;
b. an offense within the scope of the Convention for the Suppression of Unlawful Acts against the Safety of Civil Aviation, signed at Montreal on 23 September 1971;
c. a serious offense involving an attack against the life, physical integrity or liberty of internationally protected persons, including diplomatic agents;
d. an offense involving kidnapping, the taking of a hostage or serious unlawful detention;
e. an offense involving the use of a bomb, grenade, rocket, automatic firearm or letter or parcel bomb if this use endangers persons;
f. an attempt to commit any of the foregoing offenses or participation as an accomplice of a person who commits or attempts to commit such an offense.

Article 2

1. For the purposes of extradition between Contracting States, a Contracting State may decide not to regard as a political offense . . . a serious offense involving an act of violence . . . against life, physical integrity or liberty of a person. . . .

Article 5

Nothing in this convention shall be interpreted as imposing an obligation to extradite if the requested State has substantial grounds for believing that the request for extradition for an offense mentioned in Article 1 or 2 has been made for the purpose of prosecuting or punishing a person on account of his race, religion, nationality or political opinion, or that that person's position may be prejudiced for any of these reasons.

Article 6

1. Each Contracting State shall take such measures as may be necessary to establish its jurisdiction over an offense mentioned in Article 1 in the case where the suspected offender is present in its territory and it does not extradite him after receiving a request for extradition from a Contracting State whose jurisdiction is based on a rule of jurisdiction existing equally in the law of the requested State. . . .

Article 7

A Contracting State in whose territory a person suspected to have committed an offense mentioned in Article 1 is found and which has received a request for extradition under the conditions mentioned in Article 6, paragraph 1, shall, if it does not extradite that person, submit the case, without exception whatsoever and without undue delay, to its competent authorities for the purpose of prosecution. Those authorities shall take their decision in the same manner as in the case of any offense of a serious nature under the law of that State.

Article 8

1. Contracting States shall afford one another the widest measure of mutual assistance in criminal matters in connection with proceedings brought in respect of the offenses mentioned in Article 1 or 2. The law of the requested State concerning mutual assistance in criminal matters shall apply in all cases. Nevertheless this assistance may not be refused on the sole ground that it concerns a political offense or an offense connected with a political offense or an offense inspired by political motives.

2. Nothing in this Convention shall be interpreted as imposing an obligation to afford mutual assistance if the requested State has substantial grounds for believing that the request for mutual assistance in respect of an offense mentioned in Article 1 or 2 has been made for the purpose of prosecuting or punishing a person on account of his race, religion, nationality or political opinion, or that that person's position may be prejudiced for any of these reasons. . . .

Article 13

1. Any State may, at the time of signature or when depositing its instrument of ratification, acceptance or approval, declare that it reserves the right to refuse extradition in respect of any offense mentioned in Article 1 which it considers to be a political offense, an offense connected with a political offense or an offense inspired by political motives, provided that it undertakes to take into due consideration, when evaluating the character of the offense, any particularly serious aspects of the offense, including:
   a. that it created a collective danger to the life, physical integrity or liberty of persons; or
   b. that it affected persons foreign to the motives behind it; or
   c. that cruel or vicious means have been used in the commission of the offense.

BIBLIOGRAPHY

Antokol, Norman, and Mayer Nudell. *No One Neutral*. Medina, OH: Alpha Publishing, 1990.

Bassiouni, M. Cherif. *A Draft International Criminal Code and Draft Statute for an International Criminal Tribunal*. Boston: Kluwer, 1987.

———. *International Extradition and World Public Order*. Dobbs Ferry, NY: Oceana Publications, 1974.

Berkowitz, Bruce D., and Allan E. Goodman. *Strategic Intelligence*. Princeton: Princeton University Press, 1989.

Crenshaw, Martha. *Terrorism and International Cooperation*. Institute for East-West Security Studies Occasional Paper Series, no. 11. New York, 1989.

———, ed. *Terrorism, Legitimacy, and Power*. Middletown, CT: Wesleyan University Press. 1983.

Dobson, Christopher, and Ronald Payne. *The Never-Ending War*. New York: Facts on File, 1987.

Essays on Strategy. Washington, DC: National Defense University Press, 1985.

Felix, Christopher. *A Short Course in the Secret War*. New York: Dell, 1963.

Ferencz, Benjamin. *An International Criminal Court: A Step Toward World Peace*. Dobbs Ferry, NY: Oceana Publications, 1980.

Hood, William. *Mole*. New York, Ballantine Books, 1982.

Kupperman, Robert, and Jeff Kamen. *Final Warning*. New York: Doubleday, 1989.

Laqueur, Walter. *The Age of Terrorism*. Boston: Little, Brown, 1987.

Ledeen, Michael. *Perilous Statecraft*. New York: Scribners, 1988.

Manchester, William. *The Last Lion*. Boston: Little, Brown, 1988.

Martin, David, and John Walcott. *Best Laid Plans*. New York: Harper & Row, 1988.

Netanyahu, Benjamin. *Terrorism—How the West Can Win*. New York: Farrar, Straus & Giroux, 1986.

Revel, Jean-Francois, *How Democracies Perish*. New York: Harper & Row, 1983.

Richelson, Jeffrey. *Foreign Intelligence Organizations*. Cambridge, MA: Ballinger, 1988.

Segaller, Stephen. *Invisible Armies: Terrorism Into the 1990s*. San Diego: Harcourt Brace Jovanovich, 1987.

Shafritz, Jay M., et al. *The Facts on File Dictionary of Military Science.* New York: Facts on File, 1989.

Strategic Review 22, no. 4 (Fall 1989).

Treverton, Gregory. *Covert Action.* New York: Basic Books, 1987.

United States Strategic Institute. *Strategic Review.* Fall 1989.

US Department of Defense. *Terrorist Group Profiles.* 1988.

US Department of State. *Patterns of Global Terrorism.* Department of State Yearbook.

Van Creveld, Martin. *Technology and War.* New York, Free Press. 1989.

West, Nathan. *GCHQ, The Secret Wireless War.* London: Weidenfeld & Nicolson, 1986.

ABOUT THE AUTHOR

Richard Allan has been a Professor of Law at Brooklyn Law School in New York since 1973. He is also serving as the 1989–1991 American Scholar-in-Residence at the Institute for East-West Security Studies. In addition, he has worked as a litigator at the law firm of Kelley, Drye and Warren in New York, and as Assistant District Attorney in New York County. Before he became an attorney, he was a television director at CBS. Professor Allan's previous publications include *New York Family Law* (Norcross, VA: The Harrison Co., 1988) and "Demarche or Destruction of the Federal Courts," *Brooklyn Law School Journal* 40 (1975).